INTRODUCTION TO BUSINESS AND COMPANY LAW

STUDY TEXT

AQ2016

AAT Foundation Diploma in Accounting and Business – Level 2

British Library Cataloguing-in-Publication Data

A catalogue record for this book is available from the British Library.

Published by
Kaplan Publishing UK
Unit 2, The Business Centre
Molly Millars Lane
Wokingham
Berkshire
RG41 2QZ

ISBN 978 1 78740 040 5

The text in this material and any others made available by any Kaplan Group company does not amount to advice on a particular matter and should not be taken as such. No reliance should be placed on the content as the basis for any investment or other decision or in connection with any advice given to third parties. Please consult your appropriate professional adviser as necessary. Kaplan Publishing Limited and all other Kaplan group companies expressly disclaim all liability to any person in respect of any losses or other claims, whether direct, indirect, incidental, consequential or otherwise arising in relation to the use of such materials.

CONTENTS

STUDY TEXT

Introduction to Business and Company Law

Mock Assessment

INTRODUCTION

HOW TO USE THESE MATERIALS

These Kaplan Publishing learning materials have been carefully designed to make your learning experience as easy as possible and to give you the best chance of success in your AAT assessments.

They contain a number of features to help you in the study process.

The sections on the Unit Guide, the Assessment and Study Skills should be read before you commence your studies.

They are designed to familiarise you with the nature and content of the assessment and to give you tips on how best to approach your studies.

STUDY TEXT

This Study Text has been specially prepared for the revised AAT qualification introduced in September 2016.

It is written in a practical and interactive style:

- key terms and concepts are clearly defined

- all topics are illustrated with practical examples with clearly worked solutions based on sample tasks provided by the AAT in the new examining style

- frequent activities throughout the chapters ensure that what you have learnt is regularly reinforced

ICONS

The study chapters include the following icons throughout.

They are designed to assist you in your studies by identifying key definitions and the points at which you can test yourself on the knowledge gained.

 Definition

These sections explain important areas of Knowledge which must be understood and reproduced in an assessment

 Example

The illustrative examples can be used to help develop an understanding of topics before attempting the activity exercises

 Activity

These are exercises which give the opportunity to assess your understanding of all the assessment areas.

UNIT GUIDE

Introduction to Business and Company Law (IBLW)

This unit introduces students to some of the main areas of business and company law that are relevant to the work of accountants.

The purpose of the unit is to introduce some key aspects of commercial law and to show students how the law affects the role of the professional accountant on a daily basis. This unit also provides students with practical knowledge about the law that they may find useful in their personal lives as well as at work and in doing so, covers a range of different areas of law, including contract law, employment law and company law.

In contract law, students will learn how to identify a legally binding contract and the consequences of breach of contract.

In employment law, students will learn about the distinction between being employed and self-employed, and the effect that this has on both the individual and the employer. They will also learn about the duties of the employer and the employee and what can happen when a person is dismissed or made redundant.

In company law, students will learn about the implications of setting up a company and be able to contrast this with the alternatives of operating either as a sole trader or in a partnership.

This unit is intended to develop students' wider business skills and it can be taken at any time during Foundation level. However, it is worth noting that the employment law content of this unit links with Introduction to Payroll and this link may influence the best time for students to attempt this unit.

Introduction to Business and Company Law is a mandatory unit in the AAT Foundation Diploma in Accounting and Business.

Learning objectives

On completion of this unit the learner will be able to:

- Identify key elements of the English legal system
- understand principles of contract law
- identify key employment law issues
- recognise the consequences of setting up a limited company

In any one assessment, students may not be assessed on all content, or on the full depth or breadth of a piece of content.

The content assessed may change over time to ensure validity of assessment, but all assessment criteria will be tested over time.

Learning Outcomes and Assessment criteria

The unit consists of four learning outcomes. These are set out below and reference is also made to the relevant assessment criteria within the Text, in the chapter overview section at the beginning of each chapter.

1. Identify key elements of the English legal system (chapter 1)

1.1 Distinguish between different types of law

Students need to know:

- the difference between common law and equity
- the difference between public law and private law
- the difference between criminal law and civil law.

1.2 Identify the main sources of law in the UK

Students need to know:

- what is meant by the term case law and how judicial precedent works
- the difference between direct legislation (Acts of Parliament) and delegated legislation (statutory instruments, bye-laws and Orders in Council)
- the effect of EU law: difference between EU regulations and EU directives.

2. Understand principles of contract law (chapter 2)

2.1 Identify how contracts are formed

Students need to know:

- invitation to treat, offer and termination
- acceptance
- intention to create legal relations
- consideration
- capacity and legality (valid, void, voidable contracts).

2.2 Distinguish between different contract terms

Students need to know:

- the difference between terms and representations
- the difference between express and implied terms
- different types of terms: conditions, warranties and exclusion clauses.

2.3 Indicate how a contract may be discharged

Students need to know:

- discharge of a contract: by performance, by frustration, by breach (express and implied anticipatory breach, actual breach)

2.4 Distinguish between different remedies available for breach of contract

Students need to know:

- damages: normal and abnormal, liquidated damages and penalty clauses
- equitable remedies: specific performance, injunction, rescission (cancelling a contract).

3. Identify key employment law issues (chapter 3)

3.1 Distinguish between an employee (working under a contract of service) and a self-employed person (working under a contract for services)

Students need to know:

- that there are a range of tests to determine whether somebody is employed or self-employed (control, economic reality, integration tests)

- the importance of the distinction between being employed and self-employed from a legal perspective.

3.2 Identify the implied duties of an employer and an employee

Students need to know:

- the duties of an employee under common law: faithful service, to obey lawful and reasonable orders, not to misuse confidential information, to show reasonable skill and care in the workplace, personal service, trust and confidence

- the duties of an employer under common law: to provide reasonable payment for work performed, to meet employee expenses, to offer a safe place to work, to provide work, to supply references, not to disclose confidential employee information, trust and confidence

- the duties of an employer under statute: to offer equal pay, to pay national minimum wage / national living wage, to offer minimum notice periods, to operate within health and safety legislation and working time regulations, to protect employees from discrimination, to make pension contributions.

3.3 Identify the legal implications of unfair dismissal and redundancy

Students need to know:

- unfair dismissal: procedure for claiming unfair dismissal, potentially fair and automatically unfair reasons for dismissal, remedies for unfair dismissal

- redundancy: grounds for redundancy, consultation procedure process, calculating redundancy pay.

4. Recognise the consequences of setting up a limited company (chapter 4)

4.1 Identify differences between companies and sole traders and partnerships

Students need to know:

- the effect of limited liability and the consequences of a company being a separate legal entity

- the meaning of the phrase 'lifting the corporate veil' and when this can be done under both common law and statute

- key differences between companies and sole traders and partnerships (including limited liability partnerships)

- key differences between private and public companies (excluding those relating to directors' loans, payment for shares, pre-emption rights, reduction of capital and opening year rules).

4.2 Identify issues to be considered when forming a company

Students need to know:

- the registration documents required to form a company

- 'off the shelf' companies

- pre-incorporation contracts

- choice of company name: what names can and cannot be used, rules about similar and misleading names, where company names need to be displayed.

4.3 Identify the books, records, accounts and returns that a company must keep or file

Students need to know:

- statutory books that a company must keep

- accounting records that a company must keep

- annual financial statements that a company must file and filing dates

- annual returns that a company must file.

THE ASSESSMENT

The format of the assessment

Assessment will be by computer-based assessment (CBA) with a mixture of computer-marked tasks, including multiple choice, true/false, drag and drop, drop-down lists, calculation and completion of relevant forms. All tasks will be independent of the other tasks in the assessment.

The time allowed for the assessment is 1 hour 30 minutes.

The weighting of the learning outcomes is as follows:

1. Identify key elements of the English legal system	5%
2. Understand principles of contract law	35%
3. Identify key employment law issues	30%
4. Recognise the consequences of setting up a limited company	30%

KAPLAN PUBLISHING

STUDY SKILLS

Preparing to study

Devise a study plan

Determine which times of the week you will study.

Split these times into sessions of at least one hour for study of new material. Any shorter periods could be used for revision or practice.

Put the times you plan to study onto a study plan for the weeks from now until the assessment and set yourself targets for each period of study – in your sessions make sure you cover the whole course, activities and the associated questions with answers at the back of the Study Text.

If you are studying more than one unit at a time, try to vary your subjects as this can help to keep you interested and see subjects as part of wider knowledge.

When working through your course, compare your progress with your plan and, if necessary, re-plan your work (perhaps including extra sessions) or, if you are ahead, do some extra revision/practice questions.

Effective studying

Active reading

You are not expected to learn the text by rote, rather, you must understand what you are reading and be able to use it to pass the assessment and develop good practice.

A good technique is to use SQ3Rs – Survey, Question, Read, Recall, Review:

1   **Survey the chapter**

    Look at the headings and read the introduction, knowledge, skills and content, so as to get an overview of what the chapter deals with.

2   **Question**

    Whilst undertaking the survey ask yourself the questions you hope the chapter will answer for you.

3   Read

Read through the chapter thoroughly working through the activities and, at the end, making sure that you can meet the learning objectives shown within the summary.

4   Recall

At the end of each section and at the end of the chapter, try to recall the main ideas of the section/chapter without referring to the text. This is best done after short break of a couple of minutes after the reading stage.

5   Review

Check that your recall notes are correct.

You may also find it helpful to re-read the chapter to try and see the topic(s) it deals with as a whole.

Note taking

Taking notes is a useful way of learning, but do not simply copy out the text.

The notes must:

- be in your own words

- be concise

- cover the key points

- be well organised

- be modified as you study further chapters in this text or in related ones.

Trying to summarise a chapter without referring to the text can be a useful way of determining which areas you know and which you don't.

Three ways of taking notes

1   Summarise the key points of a chapter

2   Make linear notes

A list of headings, subdivided with sub-headings listing the key points.

If you use linear notes, you can use different colours to highlight key points and keep topic areas together.

Use plenty of space to make your notes easy to use.

3   Try a diagrammatic form

The most common of which is a mind map.

To make a mind map, put the main heading in the centre of the paper and put a circle around it.

Draw lines radiating from this to the main sub-headings which again have circles around them.

Continue the process from the sub-headings to sub-sub-headings.

Highlighting and underlining

You may find it useful to underline or highlight key points in your study text – but do be selective.

You may also wish to make notes in the margins.

Further reading

In addition to this text, you should also read the 'Student section' of the 'Accounting Technician' magazine every month to keep abreast of any guidance from the examiners.

The English Legal System

Introduction

The AAT Introduction to Business and Company Law unit introduces some of the main areas of business and company law that are relevant to the work of accountants. The purpose of the unit is to introduce some key aspects of commercial law and to demonstrate how the law affects the role of the professional accountant on a daily basis.

This unit also provides practical knowledge about the law that is useful in personal as well as work situations.

This first chapter will explain the three main sources of the law.

ASSESSMENT CRITERIA	CONTENTS
1.1 Distinguish between different types of law 1.2 Identify the main sources of law in the UK	1 Introduction 2 Judicial Precedent 3 Statute Law 4 Criminal Law and Civil Law 5 Public Law and Private Law 6 European Union Law: regulations and directives

1 Introduction

1.1 What is law?

 Definition

Law: The principles and regulations established in a community to maintain social order, whether in the form of legislation or of custom and policies recognised and enforced by judicial decision.

1.2 Sources of law

There are three main sources of law in the English legal system:

- **Judicial Precedent** – law which has been developed over time by judges when deciding the outcome of cases brought before the courts. These laws have evolved through the English **common law** and **equity** system.

- **Statute law** – laws made by the state through **direct legislation** and **delegated legislation**.

- **EU legislation** – treaties, regulations and directives which affect countries who are members of the European Union.

 Definition

Legislation: In its widest sense the term 'legislation' includes all methods of making law. To legislate is to make new law in any fashion.

This chapter will explain these sources and summarise the court structure, as shown in the diagram below.

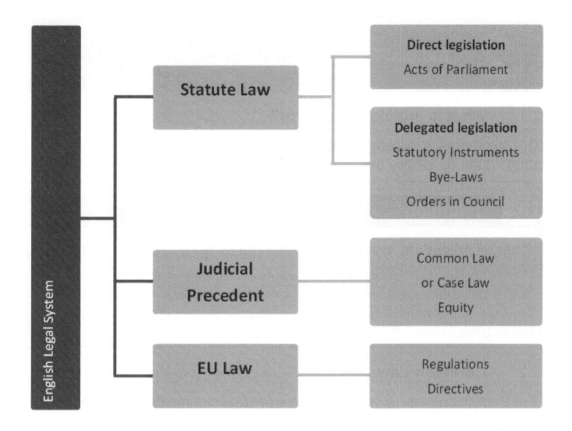

Activity 1

Identify which of the following are sources for English law.

Tick all that apply.

	Correct?
US Federal Law	
EU legislation	
AAT conceptual framework	
UK common law	
Acts of Parliament	

2 Judicial Precedent

2.1 What is judicial precedent?

The common law system developed in England and followed in many other countries follows the principle of **judicial precedent**.

 Definition

Judicial precedent is the system, adopted by judges, of following the decisions in previous cases.

Some precedents are binding (they must be followed), whereas others are merely persuasive (the judge in a later case may choose not to follow them).

2.2 Common Law

The English common law legal system evolved during the Middle Ages when the monarchy established a court system to unite both the country and its laws. Generally agreed local customs were absorbed into a body of law which could be applied to all the country: **the common law**.

One of the main features of common law is that is based on **judicial precedent**. Common law judges base their decisions on law reports from past cases where the facts are substantially the same, and so law is developed through judges' findings.

2.3 Equity

As common law courts developed, there was an increasing need for more formality. Technical requirements intensified and disputes could only be heard if they satisfied the correct legal process. This was seen to be rigid and inflexible. Also, under the common law system the only remedy available to claimants were **damages** (monetary compensation).

Courts of Equity were developed to run in parallel with the common law courts to apply principles of fairness and equity to individual cases.

Therefore equity is both more flexible than common law and more concerned with **fairness**.

Whilst common law and equity courts have now merged, in the event of a conflict between equity and the common law, equity always takes precedence.

Definition

Damages is the monetary compensation awarded by a court to an individual who has suffered the wrongful conduct of another party.

Equitable remedies are those where it is felt a monetary compensation would not be appropriate. As such, they can provide greater flexibility and are discretionary.

 Examples

Equitable remedies:

Specific Performance	The defendant is ordered to carry out their contractual duties *only if* the original contract was fair and equitable.
Injunction	A court order requiring a person to do or cease to do a specific action.
Rescission	The cancellation of a contract

 Example

An example of specific performance being used in practice:

George agrees to sell Romauld a painting for £500.

George then discovers that the painting is actually worth £5,000.

George then refuses to complete sale.

Romauld could seek a court order for specific performance against George that orders George to sell the painting to him at the agreed £500 price.

Activity 2

Complete the following paragraph using the pick list provided below.

_____ Law is a set of customs and body of rules which have developed over time to become the law of the country.

This includes past decisions made in courts, known as Judicial _____.

As only monetary remedies could be provided, over time _____ was developed to provide other remedies, including injunctions, where a Court _____ may be issued to require a person or company from taking certain actions. This particularly important in contract law.

Pick list

Equity	Common	Criminal	English	EU
Order	President	Precedent	Principle	Statute

2.4 Law reports

The outcomes of previous cases are therefore a major source of law in the English legal system. This information is found in "Law Reports". These reports explain the legal principles on which judgement was made and are referred to by other judges when they make rulings on similar cases.

LAW REPORTS

- Full text of judgement made in a case, including statement of facts and judicial reasoning
- Summary of legal issues, lists of cases cited, legislation referred to
- Two broad types: full text law reports include the full judgement, along with a summary of the case known as the headnote; summary reports (known as case notes or digests) are less detailed and formal.

Example

The internet has allowed courts to publish their decisions on websites. This is a relatively cost-effective method compared to printing the records and makes the decisions more accessible to the public and students, legal professionals and other experts.

The Incorporated Council of Law Reporting for England and Wales (CLR) is the most well-known provider of law reports in the UK, having been established in 1865. It is a not-for-profit organisation, whose case summaries are widely used.

Other online sources for Law Reports include:

British and Irish Legal Information Institute http://www.bailii.org/

The UK Supreme Court publishes the court's judgments on its website.

 Activity 3

Research any of the following recent high profile cases on Bailii:

a) *Horan v Express Newspapers [2015]* – One Direction star Niall Horan took a newspaper to court for defamation after it published a story about him and Justin Bieber.

b) *Spice Girls v Aprilia [2000]* – 1990's pop group, Spice Girls were sued by a sponsor after one of the group left.

c) *McManus v Beckham [2002]* or *Beckham v News Group News [2005]* – [1] Victoria Beckham shouts at a shop owner; [2] Rebecca Loos and disclosure request.

d) *Cosmetic Warriers [Lush] v Amazon [2013]* – Cosmetic manufacturer Lush took US giant, Amazon, to court after sponsored Amazon search links on Google for Lush products directed consumers to other brands.

e) *Murray v Express Newspapers [2008]* – Author JK Rowling takes newspaper to court after it published a picture of her son in the Sunday Express magazine without consent.

f) *McCartney v McCartney [2008]* – Former Beatle Paul McCartney's multi-million-pound divorce hearing was heard in open court.

2.5 Establishing judicial precedent

The system of following the decisions made in previous cases is called the doctrine of **judicial precedent**.

- Some precedents are **binding** (meaning they **must** be followed in later cases).

- Others are merely **persuasive** (meaning that a judge in a later case **may** choose to follow it but is not bound to do so).

Not everything said in court is binding in later cases. We have to distinguish between the **ratio decidendi** (the reason for the decision) and an **obiter dicta** – another remark made in passing (literally, 'things said along the way').

Definition

The ratio decidendi is the principle of law on which the decision is based, or the reason for deciding. It forms a binding precedent which can be carried down to determine future similar cases.

An obiter dicta is a comment or speculation made by the judge on aspects of the case. For example, the judge may discuss situations if the facts of the case were different or make more general legal comments.

2.6 Tort Law and Negligence

Previous cases can define key concepts within the law. As shown below, the case of Donoghue v Stevenson (1932) is a leading case which set judicial precedence on the legal concepts of duty of care and negligence.

Definitions

Tort comes from the Medieval Latin 'Tortus' via the French language. It was used in English to mean 'wrong'.

Tort Law is concerned with a civil wrong. For example, when one person causes damage or loss to another person or their property. Tort law can relate to cases of negligence, nuisance, trespass or defamation, but the largest area in Tort Law is negligence.

Negligence is the breach of a legal duty to take care, which results in damage to another.

For a claimant to be successful in a claim for negligence, the following essential elements must be present:

a) The defendant owed the claimant a duty of care

b) The defendant breached that duty of care

c) As a result the claimant suffered damage.

KAPLAN PUBLISHING

Definition

Duty of care is a duty owed to use reasonable care in relation to another individual and their property.

It is a duty to act the way a responsible person should act in a given set of circumstances where not acting in a reasonable manner could result in negligence.

 Example

Donoghue v Stevenson (1932)

The case of Donoghue v Stevenson 1932 is a leading case which set judicial precedent on the legal concepts of **duty of care** and **negligence**.

The Facts

The claimant, Mrs Donoghue, went into a café with a friend, who bought a bottle of ginger beer (in an opaque bottle so you could not see the contents) manufactured by Stevenson and gave it to Mrs Donoghue. Mrs Donoghue drank half of it from the bottle and poured the rest into a glass. What appeared to be a decomposing snail was found in the drink and Mrs Donoghue became ill, suffering shock and stomach pains.

The Issue

Mrs Donoghue did not buy the drink herself so she did not have a contract with the owner of the café. Mrs Donoghue's friend did have a contract with the café, but she did not become ill. Since the bottle was opaque, the café owner had no idea that there was anything wrong with the bottle.

Mrs Donoghue wanted to sue the manufacturer (Stevenson). The question was whether should be allowed. As Mrs Donoghue did not buy the bottle, she could not sue the café for breach of contract. Existing law at the time stated that you could only claim negligence if you had a contract too. Parliament had not passed legislation that set rules for negligence.

The Judgment

The House of Lords (pre-cursor to the Supreme Court, the highest court in the land) ruled 3 v 2 that the manufacturer of goods (Stevenson) owed a duty of care to Donoghue to ensure that the ginger beer was manufactured correctly.

Ratio decidendi

In Lord Atkins speech explaining the case, he stated that " *a manufacturer of products, which he sells in such a form as to show that he intends them to reach the ultimate consumer in the form in which they left him with no reasonable possibility of intermediate examination, and with the knowledge that the absence of reasonable care in the preparation or putting up of the products will result in an injury to the consumer's life or property, owes a duty to the consumer to take that reasonable care".*

Therefore Stevenson owed a duty of care not only to the buyer, but also to the eventual end user of their product.

The precedent established that where faulty products can cause harm to consumers reasonable care must be taken not to cause harm to foreseeable or potential victims.

The precedent has since become binding as it has been applied in subsequent cases in the higher courts. Once a higher court is 'persuaded' by a statement it then becomes a binding precedent.

Donoghue v Stevenson is a great example of how a previous case can impact later decisions. Many judges have relied on the judicial precedent set in this case to rule whether other defendants in other cases were also negligent.

 Activity 4

Which of the following most closely expresses the ratio decidendi of Donoghue v Stevenson?

A   A manufacturer of drinks must not deliberately put a snail in a bottle

B   Everyone must be nice to his neighbours

C   A claimant who only suffers financial loss cannot recover damages for negligence

D   A manufacturer owes a duty of care to those who he should reasonably foresee might be physically injured by his products.

 Activity 5

Although judicial precedent can lead to fairer decisions it can often be time consuming and complex due to the large number of cases to be considered.

Is this statement true or false?

3 Statute Law

3.1 What is Statute Law?

Statute Law is law made by the state (national government) to regulate behaviour within a society.

 Example

Betty is driving on a road with a speed limit of 50 miles per hour. However, she is late for work and in a rush. She therefore decides to increase her speed to 70 miles per hour.

A police officer pulls her over and she is given a speeding ticket. Betty has broken a vehicle and traffic law (Road Traffic Offenders Act 1988). This Act was established as a statute, or a law that is formally written and enacted, having passed through the legislature (Parliament).

As a result, the law Betty broke was a **statutory law**.

3.2 Direct legislation

Parliament is the supreme legal authority in the UK and only Parliament has the authority to enact any law it wishes.

Parliament examines what the Government is doing, makes new laws, holds the power to set taxes and debates the issues of the day. The House of Commons (which is elected by the public) and the House of Lords (not elected, including people who have either inherited their position or been awarded it due to their contribution to society) each play an important role in the work of Parliament.

In the House of Commons, Members of Parliament (MPs) debate Bills and then vote on them to decide whether they should become laws.

Members of the House of Lords will use their experience in business, politics and/or society as a whole to consider the advantages and disadvantages of a Bill.

To create a new law (Act of Parliament) a Bill is passed through both houses of Parliament: the House of Commons and the House of Lords, before gaining Royal Assent (when the Queen formally agrees to make the bill into an Act of Parliament).

The path of the Bill through Parliament is shown below:

First Reading	Second Reading	Committee Stage	Report Stage	Third Reading
The name of the Bill and its proposer is read out	Debate takes place and the principles of the Bill are voted upon	A smaller number of MPs consider the wording of the Bill	The Bill as amended by the Committee and is reported back to the full House	The Bill is read for the final time

ROYAL ASSENT

If the House of Commons makes amendments to the Bill, the Lords must consider them and either agree or disagree to the amendments, or make alternative proposals.

If the House of Lords disagrees with the amendments suggested by the MPs in the House of Commons, or suggests alternatives, the Bill is sent back to the House of Commons.

Due to this, some Bills may go back and forth repeatedly between the two Houses of Parliament, until both Houses reach agreement. This is known as 'Ping Pong'.

For more information about how parliament works visit www.parliament.uk

The courts cannot question the validity of an Act. However, they must refuse to apply an Act that contravenes European Union law.

3.3   Delegated legislation

The Government can make changes to a law without going through the process of passing an Act of Parliament by giving provision within the original Act for **delegated legislation**.

 Definition

Delegated legislation (or secondary legislation) is law that has been passed otherwise than in an Act of Parliament (or an Act of the National Parliaments and Assemblies of Scotland, Northern Ireland and Wales). It is usually concerned with detailed changes to the law, without the need for further Acts to be passed.

For this to occur, the original Act (or primary legislation) would have had provisions that allow for future delegated legislation to alter the law to a specified extent.

The changes made under delegated legislation range in degree from technical details, for example altering the level of a fine, to filling out the substantial details of an enabling Act.

Examples of delegated legislation:

Statutory Instruments   Statutory instruments are made by Government Ministers who have been given powers in a parent Act to authorise detailed orders, rules or regulations. Statutory instruments are usually drafted by the legal office of the relevant Government Department following consultation with interested parties.

Bye-laws   Bye-laws are made by local authorities and only apply within a specific geographic area. They are created when there is no general legislation which deals with particular local concerns.

They are approved by a secretary of state before the can come into force.

Orders in Council   In times of emergency, the Crown and Privy Council have the power to introduce delegated legislation.

3.4   Advantages and disadvantages of delegated legislation

Advantages	Disadvantages
Saves Parliamentary time	The volume involved and lack of publicity means that it is difficult to keep up with changes introduced
Access to technical expertise leaves Parliament free to consider and debate the underlying principles	Could be challenged as being undemocratic as changes are enacted without review by the elected House of Commons
Flexibility – it is quick and easy to make and to change.	

Activity 6

Which of the following statements regarding delegated legislation are correct? Tick all that apply.

Statement	Correct?
Delegated legislation must be passed in Parliament the same as direct legislation.	
Bye-laws are an example of delegated legislation.	

 Activity 7

Identify which of the following are examples of delegated legislation. Tick all the correct answers.

	Correct?
Orders in Council	
Bye-Laws	
EU directives	
Acts of Parliament	
Statutory Instruments	

4 Criminal Law and Civil Law

4.1 The differences between criminal law and civil law

Law is necessary in every society to enable the harmonious co-existence of its members. In all modern societies, legal rules fall into two fundamental categories.

CRIMINAL LAW ensures that every citizen in a society knows the boundaries of acceptable conduct. Criminal offences are considered to be an offence against the whole community, and so are prosecuted in the name of the state (or specifically, the Queen).

CIVIL LAW protects individuals against one another by specifying the rights and duties of individuals. The person who takes out the lawsuit is called the **claimant.** He or she will sue the party believed to be responsible, known **as the defendant**.

KAPLAN PUBLISHING

Because of these differences, the two legal systems are treated differently in the court system.

The main differences are summarised in this chart:

	Criminal	Civil
Court	Magistrates Court or Crown Court	County Court or High Court.
Purpose	To enforce forms of behaviour by punishing wrongdoers for offences against society.	To regulate relationships between individuals by settling disputes.
Commencement of Action	The case is brought by the police or Crown Prosecution Service (CPS) in the name of the Crown.	The case is brought by an individual who is seeking a remedy from another individual or organisation
When a case is brought against someone, they are …	Charged with an offence; prosecuted	sued
The accused is called…	the defendant	the defendant
The person starting the case is called…	the prosecution	the claimant
The case is referred to as	R v (name of the defendant) In speech this would be The Queen (R standing for Regina - Latin for Queen) against (name of the defendant)	(defendant's name) v (claimant's name)
Burden of Proof	The prosecution have to prove guilt beyond reasonable doubt (higher standard of proof)	The claimant must prove guilt on the balance of probabilities (lower standard of proof)
Outcome	Conviction or acquittal.	Defendant is liable or not liable to the claimant
Remedy	A punishment imposed by the state, e.g. a fine or a period of imprisonment.	A court order to the defendant to pay damages to the claimant, or an equitable remedy, e.g. injunction.

*It could be considered libellous to say that a defendant in a civil law case has been found guilty, as this suggests a criminal offence has been committed, rather than saying that they had lost a case in a less serious civil offence. Similarly, saying that a defendant in a civil case has been sentenced or fined would imply a more serious offence.

4.2   The criminal and civil court system

Cases progress through the court system depending on the seriousness of the crime or the complexity of the case.

All minor criminal matters are dealt with by the Magistrates Courts. Serious cases are referred up to the Crown Court where the case is heard before a jury and presided over by a judge. Appeals are heard in the Court of Appeal (Criminal Division)

Most civil cases are heard, in the first instance, by the County Court, although if large amounts of money are involved, they will be initially held in the High Court. Appeals are held in the Court of Appeal (Civil Division).

The highest court is the Supreme Court which considers appeals that concern points of law of general public importance.

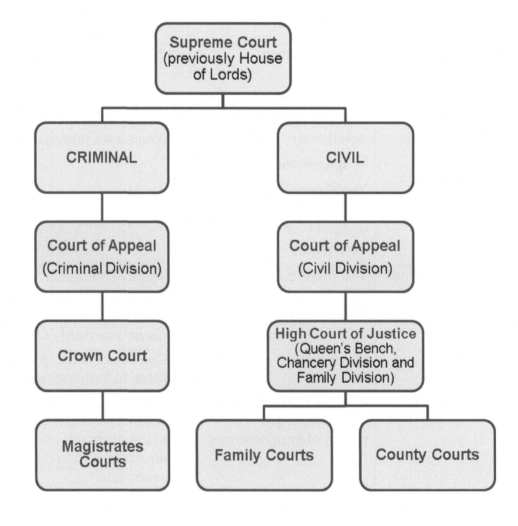

Examples – the civil courts

SUPREME COURT

The House of Lords was replaced by the Supreme Court as the highest court in October 2009 to separate legal and political powers. Normally it consists of five Justices of Supreme Court hearing appeals from the Court of Appeal and very occasionally from the High Court.

For important cases more than five judges will sit. For example, in the recent high-profile case brought by Gina Miller against the Government's proposed plan to trigger EU Article 50 *(R (on the application of Miller and another) v Secretary of State for Exiting the European Union [2017])* all eleven Supreme Court justices heard the case. The justices ruled 8 v 3 in favour that the Government must get Parliament's approval before commencing. In the appeal courts a majority vote wins the day, which is why there is usually an odd number of judges hearing the cases.

COURT OF APPEAL

Three Lords Justices of Appeal hear appeals from both the High Court and County Courts.

HIGH COURT OF JUSTICE

One High Court judge in first instance, two or three for appeals.

The High Court is split into three divisions, based on the type of claims heard.

Queen's Bench Division hear first instance cases of contract and tort. Chancery Division deals with land law, trusts, company law, insolvency, etc. Family Division hears matrimonial cases.

COUNTY COURTS

First instance civil claims in contract, tort, landlord/tenant, probate and insolvency. One district judge hears small claims, one circuit judge hears most fast-track and multi-track cases.

When a claim is received it will be allocated to one of three tracks for the hearing. The small claims track is more informal and deals with claims up to £10,000. The fast-track deals with claims between £10,000 and £25,000 expected to not last more than one day. The multi-track deals with claims of over £25,000 and/or more complex cases.

Activity 8

Which **one** of the following would be judged under civil law?

A   A prosecution for murder

B   An action by a claimant for £1 million damages for fraudulent misrepresentation

C   Proceedings where the accused is tried for the offence of applying a false trade description for goods

D   A prosecution by HMRC for non-payment of tax

 Activity 9

All criminal cases commence in

A   The County Court

B   The Crown Court

C   The Court of Appeal

D   The Magistrates Court

 Activity 10

The government department responsible for bringing criminal cases before the courts is known as _____.

Tick the correct box to complete this sentence.

	Correct?
Court Prosecution Service	
Crown Prosecution Service	
Criminal Prosecution Service	
Criminal Persecution Service	

KAPLAN PUBLISHING

5 Public Law and Private Law

5.1 The differences between public law and private law

Within the category of civil law there are two distinct areas of law: private and public law.

- **Public law** affects relationships between individuals and the state and governs the way that public authorities (e.g. local councils, government departments, services such as the police) exercise their powers. The main form of action in public law is an application for judicial review to challenge the decisions or acts of public bodies.

- **Private law** affects relationships between individuals, businesses and small groups.

 Examples

PUBLIC LAW (deals with matters relating to the whole country):

Constitutional law

Administrative law

Social welfare law

PRIVATE LAW (concerned with laws enforced between individuals):

Family law

Company law

Land law

Probate

Laws dealing with Intellectual Property rights

6 European Union Law: regulations and directives

6.1 The European Union

The European Union (EU) is an economic and political partnership involving 28 European countries. It has its own parliament which sets rules on a wide range of areas.

In 1973 the UK joined the European Economic Community (EEC), which later became the European Union. One of the requirements of entry was accepting that EEC law must be supreme across all member states. The UK Parliament enacted a statute, the European Communities Act 1972, which made EU law supreme. It states:

All such rights, powers, liabilities, obligations and restrictions ('of EEC law') are without further enactment to be given legal effect or used in the United Kingdom shall be recognised and available in law, and be enforced, allowed and followed accordingly.

Following a referendum in 2016, the UK public voted to leave the European Union. However, until the UK ceases to be a member it will continue to abide by EU treaties and laws, but not partake in decision-making. The UK will cease to be a member of the European Union in 2019.

As defined by the European Communities Act 1972, at present (prior to 2019) EU law is supreme to UK law. The UK has also established the principle of supremacy in case law giving EU law priority over national law.

6.2 Forms of European Union legislation

The main forms of EU legislation are:

Treaties	Agreements made between Member States of the European Union. Examples of other EU treaties are found below.
Regulations	These are applied in full and are binding to all member states. Regulations do not need further national legislation to be enforceable. For example, when the EU wanted to ensure common safeguards on goods imported from the EU, a regulation was adopted.
Directives	These are addressed to all member state and require national governments to enact national legislation. In the UK, directives are usually implemented by Statutory Instruments and occasionally by Acts.

Directives which affect businesses and have been enforced through UK legislation include:

EU Directive	Adapted UK legislation
Working Time Directive	The Working Time Regulations
Equal Pay Directive	The Equal Pay Act 1970 (Amendment) Regulations 2003

Decisions — These are addressed to particular member states, individuals or companies.

 Examples

EU Treaties

The idea of the European Union was established after World War II to create a community where countries would be bound together by strong economic and social ties, which would prevent further wars. The current European Union has evolved through numerous treaties since this.

The main ones are detailed here:

European Economic Community (EEC) was created by the **Treaty of Rome of 1957**. The aim of this treaty was to bring about economic integration amongst European countries including a common market and customs union to allow relatively free movement of goods and services.

In 1992, the **Treaty of Maastricht** established the single market of the European Union (EU). This single market standardised the systems of laws that applied in all member states and allowed more freedom of movement. For example, passport controls were abolished between most countries in the European Union (the Schengen Area).

The Treaty of Maastricht also established the European Monetary Union with the introduction of the euro and a single monetary policy on 1 January,1999.

The **Lisbon Treaty** is the current ruling treaty. It was signed by the heads of state and government of the then 27 EU Member States (Croatia became the 28th member in 2013) on 13 December 2007 and became law on 1 December 2009. The intention of the treaty was to make the Union "more democratic, more transparent and more efficient".

Examples

EU directives

Many of the Consumer Protection laws in the United Kingdom result from directives from the European Union. For example, Consumer Protection Act 1987 and Unfair Terms in Consumer Contracts Regulations 1999. The former addressed consumer safety relating to defective products whereas the latter protected the consumer from unreasonable terms or exemption clauses.

6.3 Human Rights Act 1998

The Human Rights Act 1998 incorporated the European Convention for the Protection of Human Rights and Fundamental Freedoms 1950 into the English legal system. The Convention sets out certain fundamental rights of the citizens of Europe, including the right to life, the right to a fair trial and the right to respect for private and family life. The Human Rights Act 1998 means that such cases can now be dealt with in the English legal system. Before the Human Rights Act, claimants had to appeal to the European Court of Human Rights for a ruling. This was very time consuming and expensive process.

It is important to note that the European Court of Human Rights and the European Convention of Human Rights are separate from EU law. The European Court of Human Rights is an international court, based in Strasbourg, France

The EU has its own court in Luxembourg (European Court of Justice). The European Court of Justice is mostly concerned with interpreting EU law and deals principally with disputes between national governments and between governments and the various EU institutions.

 Activity 11

Which form of EU legislation does the following description best describe:

These are addressed to all states and require an objective to be achieved by a certain date, which in the UK often means the use of Statutory Instruments or the passing of Acts of Parliament.

A   Treaties

B   Directives

C   Decisions

D   Human Rights Acts 1998

End of chapter activities

 Activity 12

A Parliamentary Bill becomes an Act of Parliament

A   When it passes through the committee stage

B   On receiving its third reading

C   When it reaches the House of Lords

D   On receiving the Royal Assent

 Activity 13

Which **one** of the following statements is correct?

A   The aim of criminal law is to regulate behaviour within society by the threat of punishment

B   The aim of criminal law is to punish offenders

C   The aim of criminal law is to provide a means whereby injured persons may obtain compensation

D   The aim of criminal law is to ensure that the will of the majority is imposed on the minority

 Activity 14

Which of the following statements is correct?

(i)   In the event of a conflict between equity and the common law, the common law prevails

(ii)   An Act of Parliament can overrule any common law or equitable rule.

A   (i) only

B   (ii) only

C   Neither (i) or (ii)

D   Both (i) and (ii)

Activity 15

Each of the following statements refers to either criminal law or civil law. Tick the relevant box to show which type of law is being described.

Statement	Criminal	Civil
The case is brought by the CPS in the name of the Crown		
It is intended to settle disputes between individuals		
The case will be seen before the Magistrates Court or Crown Court.		
The prosecution have to prove guilt beyond reasonable doubt.		
If the claimant wins, the defendant will be held liable for the relevant wrong.		

 Activity 16

The term 'private law' refers to which of the following:

A   The body of laws that come from the deciding of previous cases

B   The body of laws that seek to regulate the relationship between individuals

C   The legal principle that a person has the right to privacy

D   The body of laws that seeks to regulate the relationship between the State and its citizens

 Activity 17

Criminal law is a type of public law whereas contract law is a type of private law.

Is this statement true or false?

KAPLAN PUBLISHING

Answers to chapter activities

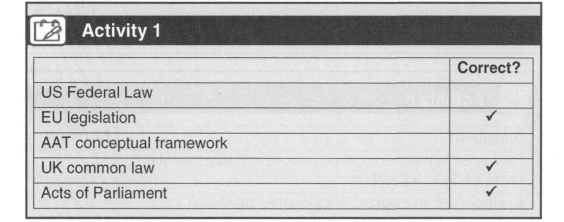

Activity 1

	Correct?
US Federal Law	
EU legislation	✓
AAT conceptual framework	
UK common law	✓
Acts of Parliament	✓

Activity 2

Common Law is a set of customs and body of rules which have developed over time and be applied as the law of the country.

This includes past decisions made in courts, known as Judicial **Precedent**.

As only monetary remedies could be provided, over time **Equity** was developed to provide other remedies, including injunctions, where a Court **Order** may be issued to require a person or company from taking certain actions. This particularly important in contract law.

Activity 3

This is a research activity.

Activity 4

The correct answer is D.

The case shows that a manufacturer owes a duty of care to those who he should reasonably foresee might be physically injured by his products.

Activity 5

The statement is true.

Although judicial precedent can lead to fairer decisions it can often be time consuming and complex due to the large number of cases to be considered.

Activity 6

Statement	Correct?
Delegated legislation must be passed in Parliament the same as direct legislation.	
Bye-laws are an example of delegated legislation.	✓

Activity 7

	Correct?
Orders in Council	✓
Bye-Laws	✓
EU directives	
Acts of Parliament	
Statutory Instruments	✓

Activity 8

The correct answer is B.

An action by a claimant for £1 million damages for fraudulent misrepresentation should be judged under civil law.

Activity 9

The correct answer is D.

All criminal cases commence in The Magistrates Court.

Activity 10

	Correct?
Court Prosecution Service	
Crown Prosecution Service	✓
Criminal Prosecution Service	
Criminal Persecution Service	

Activity 11

The correct answer is B.

This describes directives.

Activity 12

The correct answer is D.

The bill becomes an Act having received the Royal Assent.

Activity 13

The correct answer is A.

The aim of criminal law is to regulate behaviour within society by the threat of punishment.

Activity 14

The correct answer is B. Only the following is correct:

(ii)   An Act of Parliament can overrule any common law or equitable rule.

In the event of a conflict between equity and common law, equity will always prevail.

Activity 15

Statement	Criminal	Civil
The case is brought by the CPS in the name of the Crown	✓	
It is intended to settle disputes between individuals		✓
The case could be seen before the Magistrates Court.	✓	
The prosecution have to prove doubt beyond reasonable doubt.	✓	
If the claimant wins, the defendant will be held liable for the relevant wrong.		✓

 Activity 16

The correct answer is B.

The term 'private law' refers to the body of laws that seek to regulate the relationship between individuals.

 Activity 17

The statement is true.

Criminal law is public law whereas contract law typically addresses private conflicts between individuals.

KAPLAN PUBLISHING

Contract Law

2

Introduction

The law of contract is the branch of civil law which determines whether or not a promise is legally binding (i.e. enforceable by a court of law). Contracts form the basis of most commercial transactions and for this reason it is important for accounting professionals to be aware of the main elements of contract law.

ASSESSMENT CRITERIA

2.1 Identify how contracts are formed

2.2 Distinguish between contract terms

2.3 Indicate how a contract may be discharged

2.4 Distinguish between different remedies available for breach of contract

CONTENTS

1 Essential elements of a contract
2 Terms and conditions of contracts
3 Discharging a contract
4 Remedies for a breach of contract

1 Essential elements of a contract

1.1 What is a contract?

A contract is a legally enforceable agreement. It can be written, verbal or a mixture of the two. It can also be implied from the conduct of the parties. For example, all of the following everyday transactions are contracts: purchasing a newspaper; buying a bus ticket; purchasing a sandwich; buying a book or a CD.

Businesses enter into contracts each time they agree to sell or purchase goods and services. In this section we will look at the elements which make up a **valid contract**.

1.2 Valid contracts

 Definition

A **valid contract** is one which is legally binding. Therefore, valid contracts are those that meet all legal requirements.

To amount to a valid contract, the following essential elements **must** be present:

Agreement	The parties in the contract must be in agreement. One party makes **an offer** which is **accepted** by the other party to the contract.
Consideration	A two sided bargain where each side provides or promises to provide something in return for what the other is providing.
Intention to create legal relations	The parties must clearly have intended their agreement to be legally binding. For example, a social arrangement, such as an agreement with a friend to meet for a meal would not normally be treated as a contract.
Capacity	The parties must have the capacity, or ability, to contract and submit themselves to the authority of the law. For example, persons under the age of eighteen (minors) and persons of unsound mind or under the influence of alcohol have limitations on their power to contract.
Legality	A contract is not legally enforceable if it is deemed to be illegal.

We will now consider each of these essential elements in turn.

1.3   Agreement

An agreement is made when an offer has been accepted.

| AGREEMENT | = | OFFER | + | ACCEPTANCE |

It is important to understand the legal implications of these terms:

 Definition

An offer is a definite and unequivocal statement of willingness to be bound on specified terms without further negotiations.

An offerer is the party making the offer.

An offeree is the party receiving and accepting the offer.

If you make an offer it means that you are stating that you are willing to be bound to a contract in its current form with no changes required.

An offer can be in any form – oral, written or by conduct. It is made by an offerer. However, it is not effective until it has been communicated by the person making it to the recipient of the offer (the offeree).

An offer can only be accepted and hence a binding contract created if it has been **communicated** to the offeree. Communication may be either express [oral or written] or implied [through conduct].

 Example

For example, if a reward is offered for the return of a lost item, it cannot be claimed by someone who did not know of the reward before they returned the item.

An offer can be made to a specific person, to a group of people, or to the world at large.

 Example

A famous case of an offer being made to the whole world is **Carlill v Carbolic Smoke Ball Company, 1893**. The manufacturers of the medicinal 'smoke ball' claimed that anyone who bought the ball and used it as directed would not catch influenza and if they did, a reward of £100 could be claimed.

Mrs Carlill used the ball as directed and caught influenza. The manufacturers claimed that their claim was not a legal offer and even if it was, it was not possible to make an offer to the whole world, only to individuals. Likewise, they claimed that even if they could make an offer to the whole world, Mrs Carlill had not communicated her acceptance of the offer.

The court rejected these claims and stated that it was possible to make an offer to the whole world, the contract being formed with the limited number of people who accepted its terms on good faith but coming forward and buying the product. By using the smoke ball as instructed, and having purchased it under these conditions, the court also ruled that Mrs Carlill's actions had expressed an acceptance.

1.4 Termination of an offer

An offer can be terminated by:

Revocation	An offer can be withdrawn by the offeror at any time before it is accepted, even if the offeror has agreed to keep the offer open. The revocation must be communicated to the offeree, i.e. it must be brought to his actual notice. An offer cannot be revoked if the offeree has paid the offeror to keep the offer open and made part payment.
Rejection	An offeree may reject the offer outright or make a counter offer.
Lapse	An offer will lapse on: • the death of the offeror or the offeree • the expiry of a fixed time (if given) or after a reasonable time.

Once an offer has been terminated, it cannot be accepted.

1.5 Acceptance of an offer

Once an offer has been made the next stage is for the contract to be **accepted**.

 Definition

Acceptance is the unqualified and unconditional agreement to all the terms of the offer.

It must be **communicated** to the offerer by word or action.

One of the key challenges in contract law is to establish when an offer has been made and when it has been accepted.

For example, imagine you are in a shop looking to buy a magazine. Who makes the offer and who accepts? Do you make the offer to buy the magazine that the shopkeeper accepts or does the shopkeeper offer to sell you the magazine that you accept?

If the shopkeeper makes the offer to sell you the magazine, when would you accept?

(i)   When you pick up the magazine to flick through?

(ii)   When you put it in your basket?

(iii)   When you walk to the counter?

(iv)   When you stand at the till?

If any of these were correct, does this mean you cannot change your mind without breaching a contract?

Fortunately, case law helps here as this question has come before the courts. The leading case is *Pharmaceutical Society of Great Britain v Boots Cash Chemists (1953),* which concerned medicine on a counter in a shop. In this case the judge ruled that the shopkeeper accepts your offer when he takes your payment.

Logically, this must be correct. It is at this point that you are committing to buy the magazine. At every other stage, you can change your mind, turn around and put the magazine back. It would be crazy if you were entering a binding contract just by putting an item your basket.

1.6 Invitation to treat

Offers must be distinguished from other actions which may appear to be similar. An **invitation to treat**, for example, is not an offer. Technically, displays in shops are usually classed as **invitations to treat.** They do not represent offers by the shops for you to accept. Most adverts are classed as invitations to treat.

Definition

An invitation to treat is an invitation to the other party to make an offer. For example, "we may be prepared to sell Product X at Price Y".

 Example

An example of an **invitation to treat** is an advertisement, price ticket or trade price list where a written order from a customer is then the **offer.**

A frequently asked question concerns what happens when a shop prices an item incorrectly in a display. Do they have to honour it at the counter? Let us say you have had your eye on a fabulous new jacket, but the price is £79.99. One day you go into the shop and the jacket has an 'up to 50% off' sticker on it. Despite the price tag showing a price of £39.99, when the cashier runs the barcode under the scanner, it shows at the original £79.99. Can you insist they sell it to you at £39.99?

In this instance it is crucial to determine who makes the offer in a shop and who accepts. You, the consumer, makes the offer. If the shop refuses to accept your offer to buy the jacket at £39.99 then there is no contract. You cannot force them to accept.

So how does this work with websites? Does the company accept your offer when it takes your payment? Does it happen when you click 'submit'? The difficulty for online retailers is that many of these processes, including taking payment, is often automated. What if an employee accidently puts the wrong price on the item? Must the company honour the mistake?

This has happened on several occasions. Argos, famously advertised £299 televisions for £2.99 on their website, which led to one customer placing an order for 1,700 sets. Did Argos have to honour? In short, no.

Most people happily click past the terms and conditions on the way to the checkout. However, the T&C's are where the retailer tells you about contract formation. It is standard now for the retailer to state when the contract is formed.

Many retailers have changed their acceptance to when they ship your order, not when they take your money. This means if they spot the error (not difficult if somebody places an order for 1,700) before they ship, you cannot argue you had a contract and they are not obliged to sell to you at that price.

1.7 Counter offers

Of course, there is no obligation that every offeree must accept every offer they receive. If unhappy with the original offer, a counter offer can be made.

 Definition

A counter offer is an offer made in response to a previous offer. Making a counter offer automatically rejects the prior offer, and requires an acceptance under the terms of the counter offer or there is not contract.

The previous example shows Joseph making a counter offer to Benjamin.

 Example

Jurgen is a football manager. He wants to buy a footballer from Southampton FC and he offers £60 million.

The Southampton FC manager responds that he will only accept £70 million for the player.

(The Southampton FC manager has made a counter-offer for the player. This has destroyed Jurgen's original offer, which cannot now be resurrected.)

Jurgen says, "No thanks, that is too much for me to pay for the player".

The Southampton FC manager cannot now go back and accept the original offer of £60 million. That offer no longer exists. Jurgen is now under no obligation to pay £60 million. There is no contract.

Of course, Jurgen will probably happily accept the Southampton FC manager's offer to sell at £60 million, but could even at this point reduce his offer to £50 million as the player may be desperate to leave.

Counter offers can go on indefinitely. You can make a counter-offer to a counter-offer, right until somebody accepts. The key is that each counter destroys any earlier offers. The earlier offer has no legal effect.

1.8 Acceptance and "subject to contract"

Acceptance is **unconditional** agreement. This can be seen where the offeree can signal acceptance to the question "Do you accept?" by simply saying "yes". If there are other conditions attached to the acceptance (i.e. the answer is "yes, but only if…"), then it will likely be a counter offer.

Sometimes an offer is accepted on a **"subject to contract"** basis. This means that whilst an agreement has been made, there may be terms and conditions written into the contract that need to be agreed by both parties.

Therefore, the words "subject to contract" mean that the parties are not legally bound until a contract has been executed. Even though both parties have agreed terms, the matter effectively remains in a state of negotiation. Furthermore, either party can withdraw from the transaction without liability.

 Example

Joseph has a sign in his car stating, 'For Sale, £1,200'. **(Invitation to treat)**

Benjamin offers £800 to Joseph. **(Offer)**

Joseph does not accept but responds to Benjamin that the lowest he would accept is £1,000. **(Counter offer)**

Benjamin accepts that price so long as the car has a valid MOT certificate. **(Counter offer)**

This is still not an agreement as Benjamin's response has a condition that must be met.

Once Joseph proves he has a valid MOT and Benjamin accepts this certificate there has been:

- An offer (to buy/sell the car), and
- Acceptance (Benjamin approves of the certificate)

1.9   Consideration

Before a simple binding contract exists, both parties must have **agreed to provide something of value to the other.** This exchange is termed the consideration and converts the promises of the parties into bargains enforceable by the courts.

 Example

Joseph has agreed to sell his car to Benjamin for £1,000.

Joseph will be suffering the loss of his car but gaining the benefit of £1,000

Benjamin will be suffering the loss of £1,000 but gaining the benefit of the car.

Therefore, a valid agreement has been formed to provide something of value to each other.

Definition

Consideration can be defined as some right, interest, profit or benefit gained by one party, or some detriment, loss or responsibility given, suffered or undertaken by the other.

The consideration needs to satisfy one of the following criteria:

Sufficient	It must be of some value (usually monetary), even if it a minimal value. It does not have to be adequate, i.e. represent the true value of the exchange.
Legal	The exchange should not be against the law.
Timely	Consideration must not be past. It can be exchanged at the time the contract is made, or afterwards (see below).
Executed	The consideration is carried out at the time the contract is made. For example, handing over 60p and receiving a newspaper.
Executory	An exchange of promises to do something in the future. For example when there is an agreement to pay for goods 'cash on delivery'. The payment and the delivery are 'executory' – completed at a later date.

 Example

Joseph offers to sell his car to Benjamin for £1,000. Benjamin agrees to pay £1,000 for Joseph's car. There has been offer and acceptance and consideration - a simple contract has been formed.

1.10 Intention to create legal relations

If an offer is accepted, then an agreement is created, but this agreement does not automatically become a contract. If one of the parties wishes to legally enforce the terms of the agreement, he must show that there had been an intention by both parties that the agreement was to create legal relations.

There is a presumption in social or domestic agreements that legal relations are not intended. However, this can be challenged if there is evidence to suggest that the parties intended there to be a contract i.e. by signing a document. In **commercial agreements**, it is generally **assumed that relations** are intended.

1.11   Capacity and legality

Each person entering into the contract must have the mental capacity or ability to be able to do so. The following groups are considered to have limitations on their power to contract and would not be bound to the contract:

- Minors – persons under the age of 18 years old
- Persons of unsound mind
- Anyone under the influence of alcohol or drugs.

As we have seen there are five essential elements which must exist in a **valid contract**. Even if these elements exist there are some circumstances where the contract would be **invalid**. For example, a contract relating to drug dealing is against the law and any disputes between the parties would not be heard in a court of law.

1.12   Types of contracts

A **void** contract is one that **cannot be enforced by law.** An agreement to carry out an illegal act or an agreement that is impossible to carry out are examples of void contracts.

A **voidable** contract is a valid contract that can be made legally null and void by one party to the contract. A contract between an adult and a minor is an example of a voidable contract as the adult is bound by the contract but the minor is not as they are not of legal age.

 Activity 1

Which of the following are features of a simple contract?

- (i)   Offer
- (ii)   Consideration
- (iii)   Relations
- (iv)   Acceptance
- (v)   Invitation to treat
- (vi)   Intention to create legal relations

Choose from the list below:

A   All of them

B   (i), (ii), (iii), (v), (vi) only

C   (i), (ii), (iii), (iv) only

D   (i), (ii), (iv), and (vi) only

Activity 2

Raphael has a notice in his shop window saying that the books he has for sale are half price.

This is an example of:

A   Offer

B   Acceptance

C   Invitation to treat

D   Consideration

Activity 3

Barry is ordering an Indian takeaway on the telephone and says he will pay when he picks up the order.

Which of the following would constitute consideration?

A   Placing the order

B   Paying for the order

C   Saying he will pay for the order

D   Picking up the order

Activity 4

Betty is the owner of a haberdashery and put a notice in the window of her shop advertising that all fabric has 20% off. This is:

A   A completed contract

B   An acceptance of an offer

C   A contractual offer

D   An invitation to treat

Activity 5

If you are shopping in a supermarket, when is a contract formed?

A   When you put your goods in the trolley

B   When you take items off the shelves

C   When the checkout assistant takes your goods

D   When you leave the shop premises

Activity 6

A void contract is a contract that:

A   is valid

B   can be enforced by law

C   cannot be enforced by the law

 Activity 7

Sinead receives a letter from Samantha containing an order for a new suite of furniture for £1,250. Sinead e-mails Samantha confirming the order and delivery date.

Before the order is delivered, Sinead realises that the suite of furniture which Samantha wants to buy is out of stock and has been discontinued. A similar suite is available for £1,750.

Which ONE of the following statements best describes the contract?

Statement	Correct?
Samantha's letter is an invitation to treat and Sinead's e-mail is an offer. As Sinead has not accepted the offer, Samantha can change it.	
Samantha's letter is an offer and Sinead's e-mail is an acceptance. Sinead cannot deliver different goods at the new price without Samantha's agreement.	
Samantha's letter is an acceptance and Sinead's e-mail is a counter offer so Sinead can now deliver the new goods at the new price.	
Samantha's letter is an acceptance and Sinead's offer of a new suite of furniture is consideration.	

 Activity 8

Which of the following statements about consideration is NOT correct? Tick the answer from the options provided.

Statement	✔
Consideration must be sufficient	
Consideration can be a promise to do something in the future	
Consideration can be past	
Consideration does not need to be adequate	

2 Terms and conditions of contracts

2.1 Contract terms and representations

The terms of a contract define the responsibilities of the parties and the remedies available if either party is in breach of contract.

A statement, written or oral, made during the negotiations leading to a contract, may be a **term** of the contract or merely a **representation**.

A **representation** is something that is said by the offeror in order to persuade the offeree to enter into the contract. It may or may not become a term of that contract.

The distinction between terms and representations is important because, if a statement is untrue, the remedies available to the innocent party differ:

- if the representation becomes a term of the contract, the innocent party has remedies for breach of the term in the form of damages as well as equitable remedies for misrepresentation

- if, however, the representation does not become a term of the contract, the innocent party will have equitable remedies only for misrepresentation.

2.2 Express and implied terms

Terms may be **express** or **implied**.

 Definition

Express terms are those specifically inserted into the contract by one or both of the parties. They must be clear for them to be enforceable.

 Definition

Implied terms are not expressly included in the contract, but they are nevertheless still part of the contract. They may be implied by statute or by the courts.

Express terms will generally override implied terms. However, some statutory terms cannot be overridden by express agreement (for example, terms inserted by the Sale of Goods Act 1979).

Example

The **Sale of Goods Act 1979** (amended 1994) provides a number of examples of terms implied by statute. The Act applies when a business sells goods. These terms impose obligations upon a seller and can be implied into every contract of sale:

- That the seller has (or will have) the right to sell the goods (S12)
- That the goods shall correspond with any description applied to them (S13)
- Where the sale is made in the course of business, that the goods shall be both of satisfactory quality and reasonably fit for the required purpose if the seller has been made aware of this (S14)
- That the bulk will correspond with any sample (S15)

The implied terms relating to the provision of services (e.g. those supplied by a plumber, an accountant) is contained in the **Supply of Goods and Services Act 1982**. The Act provides a statutory term that 'the supplier will carry out the service with reasonable care and skill'.

As a result of the contract being breached, damages or other remedies may be sought. In sale of goods contracts, where the seller is in breach of contract the buyer can either reject the goods or claim damages for their value; where the buyer is in breach of contract the seller can remedy the situation by suing for the prices of the goods or claiming damages for non-acceptance.

In addition to this, the **Sale of Goods Act 1979** gives an unpaid seller certain rights over the actual goods:

- If the goods are in the seller's possession, they may hold onto them until payment is received.
- Where the buyer is insolvent, the seller has the right to stop delivery whilst the goods are in transit so they can be recovered.
- If the contract allows, or if the buyer is notified, the seller may rescind the contract and resell the goods if payment is not received in a reasonable time.

 Example

In the case of **Rogers v Parish (1987),** the claimant purchased a new Range Rover for £16,000. It had defects in the engine gearbox and bodywork. After several attempts at repair, the car still did not function as desired and the claimant sued.

It was judged that the car was indeed of an unsatisfactory quality and as it was a new Range Rover, this had given rise to expectations above those relating to a more modest car.

Activity 9

Gladys buys a new washing machine she saw advertised on Gr8Buys TV, a satellite shopping channel.

When the washing machine arrives, Gladys realises that it is an older model to the one she saw on the television and does not have the key features which attracted to purchase it. She also finds that the machine does not clean her clothes satisfactorily and is incredibly loud, to the point where a neighbour complained to her.

Could Gladys claim Gr8Buys TV has breached the Sale of Goods Act and if so, what is the likely outcome?

2.3 Conditions and warranties

There are two main types of terms: **Conditions** and **Warranties**.

The distinction between the types of term is important because it determines the remedies that may be available in the event of a breach in contract.

Conditions	Conditions go to the root of the contract. Non-performance of Conditions may be treated by the innocent party as failure to perform the contract. Breach can result in damages or discharge or both. Discharge entitles the innocent party to end the contract and claim damages.
Warranties	Warranties are subsidiary and therefore less important to the terms of the contract. A breach of warranty can result in damages only.

 Example

John hires a digger from Macca's Building Supplies Ltd. John tells Macca that it must be delivered on 9th October. Macca delivers the digger on 10th October. The delivery date is likely to be a **condition** of the contract. John can terminate the contract and claim damages.

John agrees with Macca Building Supplies that the digger will be delivered on 9th October by 10am. It arrives on 9th October at 10.05am. It is unlikely that arriving five minutes late will have important consequences for John. This is likely to be classed as a **warranty**. John cannot terminate the contract.

Example - Condition

Poussard v Spiers & Pond (1876)

A soprano, Madame Poussard, agreed to sing in a series of operas for Spiers. She failed to appear on the opening night and Spiers refused her services for subsequent nights.

HELD: The obligation to appear on the opening night was a condition. Spiers was entitled to treat the contract as at an end and was therefore not himself in breach by refusing her services for the remaining nights.

 Example - Warranty

Bettini v Gye (1876)

A tenor, Bettini, who agreed to sing in a series of concerts and to attend six days of rehearsals beforehand failed to appear for the first four rehearsal days. Gye, in consequence, refused Bettini's services for the remaining rehearsals and performances.

HELD: The obligation to appear for rehearsals was a warranty and therefore Bettini's breach did not entitle Gye to treat the contract as at an end. Gye was in breach of contract.

2.4   Exclusion clauses

A clause may be inserted into a contract as a term to the contract with the aim of excluding or limiting the liability of one of the parties.

In order to be valid, an exclusion clause must satisfy two conditions:

*   It must be incorporated into the contract

*   Its wording must cover the loss.

An exclusion clause can be incorporated into a contract by:

Signature	If the customer signs a document containing an exclusion clause, it will form part of the contract even if the signatory did not read or understand the document.
Notice	An unsigned document such as a ticket or notice may contain exclusion clauses. Reasonable steps must have been taken to bring it to the attention of the other party at the time the contract was made. For example, car park signs that state 'cars at left at the owner's risk'.

The validity of the clause will be tested under the Unfair Contract Terms Act 1977 which restricts the extent to which liability in a contract can be excluded. For example, an exclusion clause can never exclude liability for death or personal injury.

 Activity 10

Which one of the following is incorrect?

A   A condition is a term which the parties intended to be of fundamental importance

B   A warranty is a term which the parties did not intend to be of fundamental importance.

C   If a condition is breached, then the contract must be terminated.

D   If a warranty is breached, the innocent party cannot terminate the contract.

Activity 11

Dee Ltd has broken one of the terms of its contract with E Ltd. If that term is a warranty, which of the following is correct?

A   E Ltd may terminate the contract with Dee Ltd

B   E Ltd can avoid the contract and recover damages

C   E Ltd is entitled to sue for damages only

D   E Ltd is entitled to sue for damages or to terminate the contract.

---

3   Discharging a contract

3.1   Ways to end a contract

This section covers the different ways in which a contract can be brought to an end (discharged).

There are four main ways this can be achieved:

- by performance
- by frustration
- by breach of contract
- by agreement

3.2 Discharge by performance

A contract is usually discharged by the performance of both parties of their obligations under the contract.

The general rule is that performance must be exact and precise and that a partial performance is no performance.

 Example

Cutter v Powell (1795)

Cutter was employed on a ship sailing from Jamaica to the UK. He died before completing the journey. His wife tried to sue Powell to recover part of the wages due to her husband.

HELD: The widow was not entitled to anything because her husband had not completed the journey and there was no complete performance of the contract.

3.3 Discharge by frustration

A contract is frustrated if, after the contract is formed and through no fault of either party, something happens which renders the contract impossible to perform. In this instance, neither party is in breach of contract.

 Examples

Government intervention or illegality: after the contract was formed a law was made which made the contract illegal. For example, in times of war it can be made illegal to trade with enemy countries and therefore a contract entered into before the war was declared would be frustrated.

Destruction of the subject matter: if the subject of the contract, for example, property, is destroyed the contract is frustrated.

Non-availability of one of the parties to the contract through illness or death or other exceptional circumstances.

Example

Taylor v Caldwell (1886)

A hall was let to the claimant for a series of concerts on specified dates. Before the date of the first concert the hall was accidentally destroyed by fire. The claimant sued the owner of the hall for damages for failing to let him have the use of the hall as agreed.

HELD: Destruction of the subject of the contract (the hall) rendered the contract impossible to perform and discharged the defendant from his obligations under the contract.

A contract can only be frustrated if it becomes impossible to complete after the contract was initially formed.

3.4   Discharge by breach of contract

A breach of contract occurs when one of the parties to the agreement fails to comply, either completely or satisfactorily, with their obligations under it.

 Definitions

Actual breach is where the breach occurs on the due date for performance.

Anticipatory breach occurs where, before the due date for performance, one of the parties shows an intention not to perform his contractual obligations.

This may be:

*   **expressed** – one of the parties declares that they have no intention of carrying out their contractual obligations, or

*   **implied** – when one of the parties does something which makes subsequent performance of their contractual undertaking impossible.

3.5   Discharge by agreement

The parties may decide before either of them has performed his side of the contract that they will not perform it or that they will do something different instead.

4 Remedies for a breach of contract

4.1 Types of remedies

This section examines the remedies that may be available to any injured party as a result of a breach of contract.

As we established in the previous chapter, in common law systems, remedies can be divided into two categories: legal damages and equitable remedies.

Legal damages enable the claimant to recover monetary damages. **Equitable remedies** are granted when monetary compensation is inadequate. Where there is a conflict between legal and equitable remedies, equity will prevail.

Note that not every breach has the effect of discharging the contract and thus releasing the innocent party from his obligations:

- Breach of condition does entitle the innocent party to withdraw from the contract.
- Breach of warranty only entitles to innocent party to claim damages.

4.2 Damages

This is the basic common law remedy for a breach and takes the form of monetary compensation with the aim of putting the claimant back into the same financial position he would have been in if the contract had been performed properly.

The amount payable is known as the **loss of the bargain.** This will include the return of any money paid by the claimant plus any **consequential losses** incurred as a result of the breach in contract.

The test for these consequential losses is that they should have been foreseeable to a reasonable person, when the contract was formed.

Normal losses are damages arising from the breach of the contract. They can be identified as being *within the reasonable contemplation of the parties to the contract.* In other words, they could have been in some way expected as a consequence before the event.

Abnormal losses are out of the ordinary and were not within the reasonable contemplation of the defendant at the time of making the contract.

KAPLAN PUBLISHING

Example

Victoria Laundry (Windsor) Ltd v Newman Industries Ltd (1949)

Newman Industries contracted to sell a boiler to Victoria Laundry (Windsor) Ltd for use in the dying and laundry business. The defendant was aware that the boiler was to be used immediately, however the delivery of the boiler was delayed by five months.

The claimant sued for damages both for the loss of ordinary profit and for losses incurred because it missed out on a lucrative contract because of the delayed delivery.

HELD: Damages were awarded for the loss of ordinary profits (5 month delay) because the defendant could reasonably foresee these **normal losses.** However, as the defendant was not aware of the lucrative contract **when the contract was formed** they could not have reasonably foreseen that a breach would cause this loss and so were not liable for these **abnormal losses**.

4.3   Liquidated damages and penalty clauses

It is possible for the parties agree the amount of damages before the contract is formed. However, the parties must be careful to make sure the amount is reasonable.

A penalty clause threatens large damages for breach. The amount is often very large in relation to the expected loss. A clause is therefore considered to be a penalty clause if the stated sum is extreme when compared to the maximum loss that could happen. Where the courts find the clause to be a penalty clause it will be held to be invalid and not legally enforceable.

Example – A penalty clause?

Parking Eye v Beavis (2015)

Parking Eye Ltd managed a car park on behalf of the owners of a retail park. They had installed prominent notices that failing to comply with a 2-hour maximum stay would 'result in a Parking Charge of £85'.

Mr Beavis left his car at the car park for nearly 3 hours and received a demand for payment of £85. Mr Beavis refused to pay and argued that this fee was so high compared to the actual breach of contract that it was a penalty charge and therefore unenforceable.

This case went to the Supreme Court due to its importance and relevance for other members of the public. The Supreme Court ruled that the £85 fee was **not** a penalty charge.

The judges ruled that the high fee had two objectives:

(i)   To provide an efficient use of the available parking spaces, ensuring a flow of shoppers into the shops and preventing commuters using the spaces for long-term stays.

(ii)   To generate income for Parking Eye to run the scheme.

The fact that both Parking Eye and the shop owners had a legitimate interest in the charges was key to the decision against Mr Beavis.

The Supreme Court ruled that £85 was **no higher than necessary** to achieve the objectives.

Liquidated damages are a genuine reasonable pre-estimate of the expected loss expressly stated in the contract. The amount stated is the amount of damages claimable. There should be an explanation within the contract to show how the figures were calculated. The clause is enforceable by the court.

 Example

Dunlop Pneumatic Tyre Co v New Garage and Motor Co (1915)

The claimant supplied the defendant with tyres, under a contract which imposed a minimum retail price. The contract provided that the defendant had to pay the claimant £5 for every tyre they sold in breach of the price agreement. When the defendant sold tyres at less than the agreed minimum price, they resisted the claim for £5 per tyre, on the grounds that it represented a penalty clause.

HELD: The provision was a genuine attempt to fix damages, and was not a penalty. It was, therefore, enforceable.

4.4 Equitable remedies

Equitable remedies are granted when monetary compensation through damages is not adequate.

They are only available at the discretion of the court and include the following:

Specific Performance	Requires someone to perform their contractual obligations. For example, a painter and decorator asks for an additional payment above that agreed and refuses to complete a painting job until that payment is made. With a remedy of specific performance, the painter and decorator would be required to complete the job without additional payment.
Injunction	Orders someone to do something or not do something. For example, someone could be ordered to stop harassing another person.
Rescission	Restores each of the parties to their exact pre-contractual position.

Injunctions order a defendant not to do something. They play an important part in providing protection when damages will not be adequate. However, sometimes they can be seen to make the matter worse.

Under The European Convention of Human Rights, all individuals have the right to a private life (Article 8) and the right to free speech (Article 10). However sometimes these concepts clash.

For example, injunctions have frequently been used to attempt to stop newspapers from reporting stories because the claimant argues it interferes with their private life. We have seen this previously in the case of photographs of JK Rowling's son.

 Example

Giggs v News Group Newspapers Ltd (2012)

In April 2011, The Sun newspaper ran a story on its front page regarding a footballer having an affair with Imogen Thomas, a recent Big Brother contestant. It did not name Ryan Giggs as the footballer.

Giggs immediately took out injunctions against:

(i)   the newspaper (to stop the newspaper from naming him) and

(ii)   Imogen Thomas from Big Brother (to stop further stories).

Because of Giggs' celebrity status, he was not named in the injunction, which was called CTB v News Group Newspapers.

However, news of the injunction just increased public interest in the story and who the mystery footballer was. Giggs was named on Twitter and football fans chanted songs about 'CTB' when Giggs was playing.

In this case, Giggs' injunctions did not have the desired effect.

This is unofficially known as The Streisand Effect, named after the singer Barbra Streisand. Streisand sued a company for using one anonymous picture of her house in an online photo library of more than 40,000 photos. Before the lawsuit the photo had been viewed 6 times. The month following news of the lawsuit it was viewed 420,000 times.

Equitable remedies are not granted if:

- damages are an adequate remedy
- the claimant has acted unfairly
- the order would cause undue hardship
- the order would require constant supervision by the court
- there is undue delay in seeking the remedy.

Example

Warner Brothers Pictures Inc v Nelson (1936)

The film star Bette Davis (Miss Nelson) entered into a contract with the claimants, whereby she agreed that she would not undertake other film work or any other occupation without the claimant's written consent.

The claimant sought an injunction to restrain her from doing film work for another company in breach of this agreement.

HELD: The injunction would be granted. However, no injunction would be granted to prevent her from engaging in 'other occupations' as this would force her to work for the claimants.

Example

Page One Records v Britton (Trading as The Troggs) (1967)

The claimants, as managers of a pop group (The Troggs), sought an injunction to restrain the group from breaching their contract by engaging another manager.

HELD: As the group would have been unable to obtain an order of specific performance to compel the claimants to perform their personal services as managers, the claimants could not obtain an injunction against the defendants, as there was no mutuality between the parties.

4.5   Other common law remedies

There are three other common law remedies:

i)   Action for the price

If the breach of contract arises out of one party's failure to pay the contractually agreed price, then the creditor should bring an action to recover that sum.

If the contract is for the sale of goods, the action may only be brought if the property has passed to the buyer, unless the price has been agreed to be payable in a specific date.

ii)   Quantum meruit

Quantum meruit is a Latin phrase meaning "what one has earned".

Under this remedy, the value of the contractual work which has already been performed is measured.

This remedy is likely to be sought where one party has already performed part of his obligations and the other party then repudiates the contract.

iii)   Remedies in sale of goods contracts

Where the seller is in breach of contract the buyer has the following remedies:

- reject the goods
- claim the damages for the price of the goods

Where the buyer is in breach of contract the seller has the following remedies:

- sue for the price
- damages for non-acceptance

Activity 12

The distinction between liquidated damages v penalty clauses is important.

Identify whether the following statements are true or false.

Statement	True / False
Liquidated damages represent a genuine estimate of the loss following a breach of contract.	
Liquidated damages are unenforceable in law.	
Penalty clauses represent a genuine estimate of the loss following a breach of contract.	
Penalty clauses are unenforceable in law.	

 Activity 13

Farmer owns some land, part of which is woodland. He sells the land to Butcher, who promises in the contract that he will not cut down the trees.

One year later, Butcher does prepare to cut down the trees. Farmer seeks a remedy immediately.

What remedy from the list below is appropriate at this stage?

A   Damages

B   Specific performance

C   Injunction

D   Rescission

End of chapter activities

 Activity 14

The vast majority of contracts are 'simple'.

What is meant by the meaning of the word 'simple' in this statement?

A   The terms of the contract are set out in writing

B   The contract does not need to be in any particular form to be binding

C   The contract contains fewer than ten provisions

D   The contract is not supported by consideration

 Activity 15

Which of the following are essential elements of a valid contract:

    i)   It must be in writing

    ii) The parties must be in agreement

    iii) Each party must provide consideration

Choose from the following:

A   (i) and (ii) only

B   (ii) and (iii) only

C   (i) and (iii) only

D   (i), (ii) and (iii)

 Activity 16

Complete the sentences using phrases from the pick list below.

Express terms are _____

_____ is designed to limit liability.

Pick list

always in writing   regarded as conditions   decided quickly

terms the parties have specifically agreed   An exclusion clause

made before the offer is accepted   A counter-offer   A penalty clause

Activity 17

Dennis wrote to Mark, offering to sell him a Renoir painting for £100,000. One week later, Mark wrote back saying that he would pay that amount but not for another two months. Dennis did not respond and Mark, who decided that he wanted the painting, then heard that Dennis had sold the painting to Tom.

Was there a contract between Dennis and Mark?

A   Yes. Dennis has made a valid offer which Mark has accepted.

B   Yes. Mark's response was a request for further information and he was able to accept the offer afterwards.

C   No. Mark's response constitutes a counter-offer which effectively destroyed Dennis's original offer.

D   No. Dennis's letter to Mark constituted an invitation to treat, not an offer.

 Activity 18

Tom and Sarah visited Bath for the first time in their lives and booked into a hotel for a night. On arriving in their room, they noticed that there were many conditions of contract pinned to the back of the door, and these included clauses which excluded liability by the hotel for personal injuries or loss suffered by guests while staying at the hotel.

Tom and Sarah had never seen these conditions before.

Which one of the following statements is true?

A   Tom and Sarah are not bound by the conditions.

B   Tom and Sarah are bound by the conditions if they are fair and reasonable.

C   Tom and Sarah are bound by the conditions relating to loss of property but not those relating to personal injuries.

D   Tom and Sarah are not bound by the conditions because a hotel is never allowed to exclude its own liability in contract.

Activity 19

In the event of a breach of contract, the difference between a condition and a warranty is important because it determines:

A   The measure of damages available to the innocent party

B   The type of damages available to the innocent party

C   The remedy available to the innocent party

D   Whether or not the court will exercise its discretion to grant specific performance

 Activity 20

Beryl enters a shop to purchase a new dress. She tells the shop assistant that she would like to buy the blue dress that is displayed in the shop window and priced at £100.

The assistant removes the dress from the window for Beryl, but when she tries to pay for it at the till, the manager informs her that it is not for sale.

He tells her that the dress is for display purposes only.

Choose the correct answers from the options provided to complete the following sentences:

Beryl **(is / is not)** entitled to the dress because the display of the dress in the shop window constitutes an **(invitation to treat / offer to sell)** and not an **(invitation to treat / offer to sell)**.

It follows that Beryl **(does not have / does have)** a contract with the shop owners and that the shop owners **(have / have not)** acted in breach of contract.

Activity 21

Complete the following sentences using the pick list provided:

The remedy which requires a person to carry out his contract is known as _____. The remedy requiring a person not to act in breach of contract is known as an _____. These are both _____ remedies and, as such, are discretionary. If the contract contains a provision which is designed to frighten the other party into completing the contract by setting down a disproportionate sum payable in the event of a breach, the provision will be regarded as a _____ clause and will be treated as _____, that is, of no legal effect.

Pick list:

specific performance	penalty	equitable	legal
injunction	valid	void	exclusion

Answers to chapter activities

 Activity 1

The correct answer is D.

(i), (ii), (iv), and (vi) are all necessary for a valid contract.

 Activity 2

The correct answer is C.

The notice is an example of an invitation to treat.

 Activity 3

The correct answer is C.

Saying he will pay for the order constitutes consideration.

 Activity 4

The correct answer is D.

Betty's sign showing 20% off is an invitation to treat.

 Activity 5

The correct answer is C.

The contract is formed when the checkout assistant processes your order.

 Activity 6

The correct answer is C.

A void contract is a contract that cannot be enforced by the law

Activity 7

Statement	Correct?
Samantha's letter is an invitation to treat and Sinead's e-mail is an offer. As Sinead has not accepted the offer, Samantha can change it.	
Samantha's letter is an offer and Sinead's e-mail is an acceptance. Sinead cannot deliver different goods at the new price without Samantha's agreement.	✓
Samantha's letter is an acceptance and Sinead's e-mail is a counter offer so Sinead can now deliver the new goods at the new price.	
Samantha's letter is an acceptance and Sinead's offer of a new suite of furniture is consideration.	

Activity 8

Statement	✓
Consideration must be sufficient	
Consideration can be a promise to do something in the future	
Consideration can be past	✓
Consideration does not need to be adequate	

Activity 9

Gladys has two reasons to claim that Gr8Buys TV has breached the Sale of Goods Act:

She bought the washing machine based on the description given on television. As she received a different model with less features, the description given is inaccurate.

In addition, the washing machine does not appear to be of satisfactory quality, as it fails to clean clothes and makes an unhealthy noise.

Gladys should be able to return the machine for a replacement or refund.

Activity 10

The correct answer is C.

Although if a condition is breached, the contract may be terminated, it does not need to be. The other three statements are correct, by definition.

 Activity 11

The correct answer is C. E Ltd is entitled to sue for damages only.

 Activity 12

Statement	True / False
Liquidated damages represent a genuine estimate of the loss following a breach of contract.	True
Liquidated damages are unenforceable in law.	False
Penalty clauses represent a genuine estimate of the loss following a breach of contract.	False
Penalty clauses are unenforceable in law.	True

 Activity 13

The correct answer is C.

An injunction is the best remedy for Farmer as it can also be obtained quickly. He has not suffered any damage yet and is too late to rescind the contract. Specific performance is an order to do something, whereas he needs an order not to do something (an injunction).

 Activity 14

The correct answer is B.

Most contracts are binding irrespective of their form and in this respect are described as 'simple'.

As a contract is only recognised where consideration is provided by both parties, statement D cannot be correct.

Activity 15

The correct answer is B.

A valid contract does not need to be in writing.

 Activity 16

Express terms are **terms the parties have specifically agreed**

An exclusion clause is designed to limit liability for breach of contract.

 Activity 17

The correct answer is C.

Mark's response constitutes a counter-offer which effectively destroyed Dennis's original offer.

Mark did not accept the offer and he did not request further information. Dennis's language suggests a definite offer is being made, so this would not be considered an invitation to treat rather than an offer.

 Activity 18

The correct answer is A.

Tom and Sarah are not bound by the conditions as they were not aware of them when reaching an agreement to stay at the hotel. Therefore any questions regarding fairness or otherwise of the conditions is not relevant. The hotel could have excluded liability by contract, but would not be judged to have done so in this case.

 Activity 19

The correct answer is C.

A breach of warranty only allows for damages as a remedy.

Activity 20

Beryl **is not** entitled to the dress because the display of the dress in the shop window constitutes an **invitation to treat** and not an **offer to sell**.

It follows that Beryl **does not have** a contract with the shop owners and that the shop owners **have not** acted in breach of contract.

 Activity 21

The remedy which requires a person to carry out his contract is known as **specific performance**. The remedy requiring a person not to act in breach of contract is known as an **injunction**. These are both **equitable** remedies and, as such, are discretionary. If the contract contains a provision which is designed to frighten the other party into completing the contract by setting down a disproportionate sum payable in the event of a breach, the provision will be regarded as a **penalty** clause and will be treated as **void**, that is, of no legal effect. If one party has completed his contractual obligations, all that remains is to sue for the price, in which case the remoteness of damage and mitigation of loss are **irrelevant**.

Employment Law

Introduction

In this chapter, you will learn about the distinction between being employed and self-employed, and the effect that this has on both the individual and the employer. You will also learn about the duties of the employer and the employee and what can happen when a person is dismissed or made redundant.

ASSESSMENT CRITERIA
3.1 Distinguish between an employee (working under a contract of service) and a self-employed person (working under a contract for services)
3.2 Identify the implied duties of an employer and an employee
3.3 Identify the legal implications of unfair dismissal and redundancy

CONTENTS

1   Employment status: employed or self-employed?
2   Employer duties
3   Employee duties
4   Unfair dismissal and redundancy

1   Employment status: employed or self-employed

1.1   Employed or self-employed?

In the previous chapter we looked at contracts. A further relationship which is contractual is that between the employer and the employee.

There are two types of working relationships within law:

Employee	An employee is an individual who has entered into or works under a contract *of* service for an employer.
	The majority of people in work are employees. You're classed as an employee if you're working under a contract of employment. A contract need not be in writing - it exists when you and your employer agree terms and conditions of employment.
Self-employed/ contractor	A self-employed person works under a contract *for* services to several clients/customers.
	A person is self-employed if they run their business for themselves and take responsibility for its success and failure and they are not paid through a PAYE system.

This distinction in working relationships is important as it helps to determine employees' rights and entitlements, and employers' responsibilities. It also affects how tax and National Insurance contributions are collected.

> ### Example
>
> The type of working relationship has a number of consequences:
> - Employees receive statutory protection and certain state benefits (e.g. statutory sick pay)
> - Employees are protected by Acts of Parliament which cover employment legislation
> - An employer is often liable for the acts of employees when they act in the course of the employer's business, but would not be for the acts of contractors
> - Employees receive their pay net of income tax and National Insurance under the PAYE system. Self-employed people are paid gross and are responsible for paying their own tax and national insurance contributions

Definition

A **contract of employment** is a contract **of** service whether expressed in writing or verbally or implied. The contract begins when the individual agrees to work for another in return for remuneration. However, legally the major terms of an employment contract must be written down.

All employees are entitled to a **written statement** of the major terms of the contract by the end of the second month following the commencement of employment. A written statement is not the same as a contract but is strong evidence of the contract terms.

1.2 Tests to determine employment

A variety of tests can be used to determine whether an individual is employed or self-employed. These include:

- the Control Test
- the Integration Test
- Economic Reality Test

In order to discover the true status of a worker, the courts will look at all of the circumstances and take all factors into account.

1.3 Control

Control refers to the extent to which the employer decides what tasks are undertaken and how they are performed by the employee/contractor.

The following questions can be asked to determine whether there is a right of control.

- Has the employer control or direction over the employee?
- Can he dictate time and place of employment?
- Can he dictate the method and manner of its performance?
- Is the employee subject to the employers control in a sufficient degree to make a master – servant relationship?

The answer to the above will determine if the worker is employed or self-employed:

- Yes – the earner is probably employed
- No – the earner may be self employed

1.4 Integration

Integration is the extent to which the employee is an integral part (i.e. part and parcel) of the organisation.

For example, an employee will be integrated into the business of their employer where they are provided with their own desk, a designated computer terminal at which to work, access to normal employee facilities and have unrestricted access to the employer premises. Often ownership of tools, equipment and other similar resources is used to judge this.

The problem with this test is that someone could be a self-employed contractor as well as an integral part of the organisation. For example, a doctor could be a vital part of the organisation but still be a contractor at the same time.

1.5 The economic reality test (or multiple test)

This test involves asking whether the person who is doing the work is doing so as a person in business on his own account.

Relevant factors are:

- control
- provision of own equipment
- whether he hires his own helpers
- the degree of financial risk the worker undertakes
- the degree of responsibility he bears for investment and management
- the extent to which he has an opportunity of profiting from sound management in the performance of his task
- whether there is a regular, consistent method of payment
- whether the person works regular hours
- whether there is a mutuality of obligations.

No single test is really capable of determining employee status. Therefore all of the above will need to be considered and the court will weigh up the various factors accordingly. This is shown in the following two examples of the economic reality/multiple test.

Example

Ready Mixed Concrete (South East) Ltd v Minister of Pensions & National Insurance & Others (1968)

In this case, the driver of a lorry had a contract with a company under which he drove his own lorry only on company business, obeyed a company foreman and wore a company uniform.

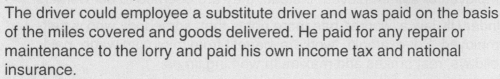

Although he provided his own lorry, it was painted in company colours.

The driver could employee a substitute driver and was paid on the basis of the miles covered and goods delivered. He paid for any repair or maintenance to the lorry and paid his own income tax and national insurance.

The Minister of Pensions claimed that he was an employee and therefore the company was required to make National Insurance contributions on his behalf.

HELD: Although the employer exercised some control over his work, the driver was not deemed to be an employee but instead an independent contractor. In particular, the fact that he owned his own equipment, operated at his own financial risk, did not have a regular wage and employed his own staff suggested he was a self-employed 'small businessman'.

 Example

Market Investigations Ltd v Minister of Social Security (1969)

A market research interviewer worked on and off under a series of contracts where she interviewed people based on instructions and questions issued by the company. She had no specified hours of work but was instructed to complete the tasks by a deadline. There was no holiday or sick pay and she could work for other companies too.

HELD: The company did have some control over the manner and time she did her work and the terms of the contract were consistent with a contract of service. The court emphasised that she did not provide her own tools or take any risk and in that sense was not in 'business on her own account'. Therefore she was not an independent contractor and could be considered to be under a contract of service.

1.6   Workers and the 'gig economy'

The introduction of new technology and working practices often raise new legal issues.

The modern concept of a 'gig economy' suggests that individual is paid for each 'gig' they complete rather than receiving a fixed monthly or weekly wage. Similarly, zero-hour contracts do not give the worker any guaranteed hours per week.

This raises the question of whether these individuals are employees or self-employed. Although it depends on the nature of the agreement between the parties, as a general rule, people working under zero-hour contracts or on a job-by-job basis are usually not considered to be either employed or self-employed. Instead, they are deemed to be 'workers'.

Under UK law a 'worker' has more rights than somebody who is self-employed. For example, 'workers' benefit from minimum wage, paid holidays, rest brakes and maximum working times.

The below chart gives a summary of some of the rights each category of worker benefits:

	Employee	Worker	Self-employed
Unfair dismissal	✓		
Redundancy	✓		
Statutory sick pay	✓		
Flexible working request	✓		
Minimum wage	✓	✓	
Paid holiday	✓	✓	
Maximum working time per week	✓	✓	
Wrongful dismissal	✓	✓	

As seen below, where mobile applications offer services over vast geographical areas, such as the transportation services company Uber, the individuals involved have been determined to be workers, rather than either employees of the company or self-employed contractors.

KAPLAN PUBLISHING

Example

Aslam and others v Uber BV and others (2016)

Uber (a technology company providing mobile apps to enable consumers to find local transportation and delivery company) claimed its drivers were self-employed and that Uber simply provided a "technology platform" that enabled drivers and users to schedule transportation.

The claimants claimed that Uber managed and controlled their activities and as such they should be regarded as "workers".

The drivers argued that they had a contractual relationship with Uber. They were interviewed by Uber before they could start and Uber controlled key information about the customers, including their names and processed payments.

The drivers did not have any direct contractual relationship with the customer. The drivers were paid weekly by Uber, who took a service fee of 20-25% from every ride. Uber could block them from accessing the app for poor performance and reserved the right to change the driver's contractual terms without agreement. Consistent poor performance could result in their account being deactivated.

HELD: The employment tribunal held Uber 'recruited, instructed, controlled, disciplined and, where it saw fit, dismissed drivers'. The drivers clearly worked 'for' Uber and therefore should be regarded as 'workers'.

 Activity 1

Which of the following statements suggest that John is an independent contractor in relation to the work he carries out for Harding Ltd?

i)   He is required to provide his own tools

ii)   He is required to carry out his work personally and is not free to send a substitute

iii)   He is paid in full without any deduction of income tax.

Choose from the list below:

A   (i) and (ii) only

B   (ii) and (iii) only

C   (i) and (iii) only

D   (i), (ii) and (iii)

Activity 2

Harding Ltd carries on its business using both employees and self-employed contractors. It is important for Harding Ltd to be able to distinguish between its employees and self-employed contractors for a number of reasons.

Which of the following reasons is incorrect?

A   Employees have a right to paid holiday, but this does not apply to self-employed contractors.

B   Harding Ltd must deduct income tax and national insurance contributions from the wages paid to its employees, but not from the amount paid to self-employed contractors.

C   Both employees and self-employed contractors can enforce contractual rights against Harding Ltd.

D   Harding Ltd must give statutory notice of terms of work to employees but not to self-employed contractors

 Activity 3

Which of the following is a test to determine a worker's status?

A   The control test

B   The reasonableness test

C   The performance evaluation

D   The liability test

 Activity 4

Indira works at Murphy's Muffins Ltd. Which one of the following factors is consistent with her being treated as self-employed?

A   Indira's employer deducts tax at source

B   Indira wears a Murphy's Muffins apron at work

C   Indira is entitled to holiday pay from Murphy's Muffins

D   Indira provides her own car for delivering cakes to offices

2 Employer duties

2.1 Employer and employee duties

Every business has a responsibility to ensure it follows the relevant rules and regulations.

This section explains the essential rights and responsibilities for every employer and employee, starting with the employer's duties towards their employees.

2.2 Employer duties under common law

Under common law, employers have the following implied duties:

- to offer reasonable payment (remuneration) for work performed
- to indemnify the employee (i.e. to offer compensation for any loss) and to meet expenses incurred whilst acting on the employer's behalf
- to offer a safe system of work. i.e. selection and supervision of staff; ensuring premises, plant and materials are safe
- to provide work. For example, if the contract is for remuneration on a piecework or commission basis, it may be possible to imply a duty on the employer to provide sufficient work to enable to employee to earn a reasonable amount. Also, an employee must be allowed to maintain their skills by practice.
- to pay the employee Statutory Sick Pay (SSP). If an employee is absent due to illness for more than 4 days and is earning more than £112 per week before deductions, the employer must pay SSP. SSP is paid for the first twenty-eight weeks of absence but generally excludes the first three days of sickness.
- to make pension contributions on the employee's behalf
- to give reasonable notice of termination of employment
- to supply references, which must be truthful (although there is no duty to provide a reference for all staff, truthful references must be supplied where required)
- not to disclose confidential employee information
- to maintain trust and confidence.

Example

Duty to provide work: William Hill Organisation Ltd v Tucker (1998)

Tucker worked as a senior, specialist dealer operating in the world of spread betting. He served notice to terminate his contract in order to work for a competitor. He remained on the payroll at William Hill but was put on 'garden leave' (he was not required to work for the company during this period but likewise could not work for anyone else). However he sought to start his new work immediately, claiming that William Hill was in breach of contract for refusing to allow him to work.

HELD: William Hill was considered in breach by not providing work because Tucker had particular, specialised skills which must be exercised to maintain them.

 Definition

Garden leave is a contractual term that allows an employer to pay an employee for the remainder of their contract without providing work. It is called garden leave as the employees are believed to spend the time working on their gardens instead.

The reason companies take this option, especially with senior staff or creative employees (such as designers) is the risk that during their notice period (which could be anywhere between 30 days and 6 months) they could access key information and use this if working for a competitor in the future.

 Example

Duty to provide a reference: Spring v Guardian Assurance (1994)

The claimant was dismissed after his previous employer was taken over by Guardian Assurance. Having applied for a job at Scottish Amicable, the claimant received a reference so bad from Guardian Assurance that the judge suggested it would be a 'kiss of death' to his career in insurance. The claimant claimed damages for negligent misstatement.

HELD: The defendants were found to be in breach of their duty to provide a reference, having issued one that might damage the employee's prospects of future employment.

2.3 Employer duties under statute

The following regulations have been passed through Acts of Parliament and protect the rights of workers under statute law.

Employment Rights Act 1996	Includes: • the right to a written contract of employment* within two months of starting employment • the right to a **minimum period of notice** to terminate the contract • protection against unfair dismissal • right to compensation [redundancy payment] if the job becomes obsolete
Equality Act 2010	Protects people from discrimination. In the workplace, this includes offering equal employment terms such as: • **equal pay** • equal holiday entitlement and sick leave • recruitment • terms and conditions • redundancy and dismissal • benefits (this builds upon the Equal Pay Act 1970, Sex Discrimination Act 1975, Race Relations Act 1976, Disability Discrimination Act 1995 and Sex Discrimination Regulations 2008).
Working Time Regulations 1998	Limits the hours of work to: • an average of 48 hours a week and gives the right to: • four weeks paid leave a year • one day off each 7 day week
Health and Safety at Work Act 1974	Employers' duties include • providing a safe system and place of work; • providing safe equipment, plant and machinery; • recruiting staff who are safe and competent • carrying out risk assessments to eliminate or control risks; • providing instruction, training and supervision to inform workers about potential hazards; • providing adequate facilities for staff welfare at work.

National Minimum Wage Act 1988 / National Minimum Wage (Amendment) Regulations 2016	Imposes minimum levels of pay for most workers: • **National Minimum Wage -** the minimum pay per hour for workers up to 24yrs old. The rate is dependent on a worker's age and if they are an apprentice • **National Living Wage** – a national rate set for people aged 25 and over. The minimum rates of pay are reviewed every April.
Employment Act 2008	Gives parents of children under seventeen or disabled children under eighteen the right to request **flexible working arrangements**. This Act also introduced paternity and adoption leave.
Pensions Act 2008	Employers have to have an automatic enrolment scheme in place into which eligible jobholders can be enrolled. There are three alternatives: • Provide an occupational pension scheme - which can either be defined contribution or defined benefit. • Use a personal pension scheme. • Use the National Employment Savings Trust (NEST). This is a low cost scheme that has been established by the Government to ensure that all employers have access to a pension provider.

2.4 Contract of employment

All employees of a company should have a contract of employment. The contract will feature a series of terms relating to both the employer and the employee, and will consist of:

• Express terms (agreed by the two parties)
• Terms implied by the courts (see the above common law duties of the employer)
• Terms implied by statute (listed in section 2.3)

Express terms are those agreed by the two parties themselves and can be written or oral. As stated previously, the Employment Rights Act 1996 requires an employer to provide an employee with a written statement of prescribed particulars of their employment within two months of the commencement of employment.

The principal written statement must include details of:

• the business's name
• the employee's name, job title or description of work and start date
• if a previous job counts towards a period of continuous employment
• the rates of pay

- the frequency of pay
- hours of work (and if week-end work and/or overtime is applicable)
- place of work (and possible relocation)
- holiday entitlement (and if this includes public holidays)

A further written statement must also contain information about:

- how long a temporary role is expected to last
- the end date of a fixed term contract
- the length of notice
- collective agreements
- details of disciplinary and grievance procedures

The statement is not a contract unless both parties agree.

 Activity 5

According to common law an employer has an implied duty:

A   To provide facilities for smokers

B   To obey lawful and reasonable orders

C   To pay reasonable remuneration

D   To adhere to the Equality Act 2010

 Activity 6

An employee is entitled to a written statement of employment particulars:

A   Immediately on commencing employment

B   Within one month of commencing employment

C   Within two months of commencing employment

D   Within three months of commencing employment

Activity 7

Which of the following would NOT be included in the written statement of employment according to the Employment Rights Act 1996:

A   The job title

B   Formal qualifications

C   Hours of work

D   The length of notice required

 Activity 8

Which of the following statements is correct?

A   An employer is obliged to provide a safe system of work.

B   An employer is obliged to give employees two days off a week.

C   An employer is obliged to provide staff with uniform.

D   An employer is obliged to provide a positive reference for all staff.

2.5   Statutory pay entitlements

As detailed above, employees benefit from a number of statutory pay entitlements. For example, if an employee is off work sick, that employee may be entitled to statutory sick pay (SSP). However, the employer may have their own occupational sick pay scheme and the employee will need to meet those requirements.

For more information on Statutory Sick Pay (including rates, examples and explanations) log on to **www.gov.uk/statutory-sick-pay**

Likewise, an employee who is pregnant may be entitled to statutory maternity pay (SMP). SMP is payable for a maximum period of 39 weeks. This period is known as the 'maternity pay period' (MPP).

The employer may provide its own maternity pay and conditions. The pay and conditions cannot be less than the statutory ones, but can provide much better conditions such as full pay for the first six months or other benefits. In these cases the employee must conform to the contractual conditions and follow the organisation's procedures.

Statutory paternity pay (SPP) may also be payable to the:

- father

- husband or partner of the mother (or adopter)

- child's adopter.

2.6   Annual leave entitlements

All employees are also entitled to annual leave. This entitlement means that their employer must honour a minimum number of paid holiday days per year.

For full time employees, this minimum entitlement is 28 days. This includes eight Bank Holidays per year in the UK. Often a new employee will start at the minimum allowed and this will increase every full year they are employed until the maximum set by the company is reached.

 Example

If an employee works 2 days a week then they will be entitled to 2 days/5 days x 28 days = **11.2 days.**

3   Employee duties

3.1   Employee duties implied by the courts

As we have seen above, the contract of employment is agreed by the two parties involved, the employer and the employee. We have established that although there are express terms, often through a written statement, which clarify the nature of the individual's employment, employers are also subject to a number of duties implied by the courts or from statute law.

As part of the employment contract, through common law there are also numerous employee duties implied in the employment contract. These include:

- they duty of mutual co-operation
- to give honest and faithful service
- to obey lawful and reasonable orders
- not to misuse confidential information
- to show reasonable skill and care in the workplace
- to give a personal service (not to delegate work unless they have the employer's permission to do so)

3.2 The duty of mutual trust and confidence

For the employer, this means giving reasonable instructions and not acting in a manner to damage the trust and confidence between them and the employee. For the employee, it requires working to ensure that the commercial objectives of the employer are not frustrated.

 Activity 9

Which of the following is NOT a duty owed by an employee towards their employer under common law?

A   A duty not to misuse confidential information

B   A duty to provide faithful service

C   A duty to maintain trust and confidence

D   A duty obey all orders given to them by the employer

4 Unfair dismissal and redundancy

4.1 Notice periods

An employee's employment may be terminated either by the employee or the employer by giving notice.

The following information regarding reasonable notice periods will be provided to you in the AAT assessment:

Notice periods

Under the Employment Rights Act 1996 (ERA 1996), reasonable notice is determined according to the length of an employee's continuous employment with the same employer as follows:

Length of continuous employment	Statutory minimum notice period
Between 1 month and 2 years	1 week
Between 2 and 12 years	1 week for each year of continuous employment
12 years or more	12 weeks minimum

Redundancy pay

Individuals may be eligible for redundancy pay if certain conditions are met. If these conditions are met, they will receive:

- 1 ½ week's pay for each year of employment after their 41st birthday.
- 1 week's pay for each year of employment after their 22nd birthday.
- ½ week's pay for each year of employment up to their 22nd birthday from the age of 18.

If termination of employment is agreed and mutual, it is not to be considered unfair dismissal.

4.2 Unfair dismissal

Unfair dismissal is a statutory right under the Employment Rights Act 1996. Only employees can bring an action for unfair dismissal (neither self-employed contractors nor "workers" qualify), claiming that the employer has terminated the contract without justifiable reason.

The following process will be followed:

The employee must have been continuously employed for two years

↓

The employee must serve a grievance notice on the employer

↓

The claim must go to the tribunal within three months of dismissal

↓

The employee must prove they were dismissed

↓

The employer must prove the reason for dismissal

↓

The tribunal must be satisfied that the employer acted reasonably

↓

If found unfair, entitlement to reinstatement, re-engagement or compensation.

4.3   Wrongful dismissal

A claim for wrongful dismissal is a common law action for breach of contract. The claim is available to both employees and independent contractors, and occurs when an employer terminates the contract

- without giving proper notice, or
- during its fixed term.

Dismissal without prior notice is known as summary dismissal. Summary dismissal is usually wrongful dismissal unless the employee:

- waives their rights or accepts payment in lieu of notice
- repudiates the contract themselves or is in fundamental breach (e.g. refusal to obey orders, serious negligence, gross misconduct)

An individual who believes they have been wrongfully dismissed may sue in the County court or High Court for damages. The limitation period for such a claim is six years.

Alternatively, if an employee, they can bring a claim to the employment tribunal provided they do so within three months of dismissal and the claim is for £25,000 or less.

4.4   Constructive dismissal

Normally employees who resign deprive themselves of the right to make a claim for redundancy or unfair dismissal. However the Employment Rights Act 1996 covers situations where 'the employee terminates the contract with, or without, notice in circumstances which are such that he or she is entitled to terminate it without notice by reason of the employer's conduct'. This is known as constructive dismissal.

Where such a repudiatory breach occurs the employee resigns and will have an action against the employer for wrongful dismissal.

 Example

Donovan v Invicta Airways (1970)

The employer put pressure on the employee, an airline pilot, to take abnormal risks on a flight. The employer did this three times in quick succession.

Each time the employee refused, causing relations with the management to deteriorate. He left the company.

HELD: The employer had committed a serious breach of contract amounting to constructive dismissal due to putting the pilot in this position. The employee succeeded in an action for wrongful dismissal.

 Example

Kevin Keegan v Newcastle United Football Club (2010)

A football club manager resigned from his position and claimed constructive dismissal. He stated that when he was appointed he was told that he would have the final say on all transfers of players into the club. The club, he claimed, had breached this term by signing a player against his wishes and Keegan said he 'had no option but to resign'.

HELD: The manager had been constructively dismissed and was awarded approximately £2 million in damages.

4.5 Automatically unfair reasons for dismissal

There are some reasons for dismissal which are automatically unfair. This means that there is no need to meet the length of employment condition.

Some examples of these reasons are:

- dismissal for requesting a written statement of terms and conditions of employment or the assertion of other statutory rights (e.g. the exercise of paternity leave rights)

- dismissal because of discrimination

- dismissal relating to maternity, pregnancy or the exercise of maternity leave rights

- dismissal relating to trade union membership/non-membership/activities
- Unfair selection for redundancy.

A further inadmissible reason for dismissal is the victimisation of health and safety complainants or whistle-blowers. A whistle-blower is a person who raises a concern about wrongdoing occurring in an organisation.

4.6 Potentially fair reasons for dismissal

Dismissal for one of the following reasons is fair unless the employer acted unreasonably in dismissing for the reason given:

- capabilities/qualifications of employee
- conduct of employee (examples of employee misconduct could include violence, theft or a serious breach of health and safety)
- redundancy
- continued employment would contravene statute law
- some other substantial reason.

An employer can only rely on a given reason for dismissal where he knew of it at the date of the dismissal.

 Example

Stevenson v Golden Wonder Ltd (1977)

A technical manager took part in an unprovoked assault on another employee at a company social function held outside working hours in the company canteen.

HELD : This was a fair reason for the dismissal, it was serious misconduct.

Once the employee has shown they were dismissed and the employer has shown that it was for one or more of the five fair reasons it is then for the tribunal to decide whether the dismissal was fair or unfair.

The reasons for dismissal need to be proved by the employer.

4.7 Remedies for unfair dismissal

Claims for unfair dismissal are heard at Employment Tribunals. This is an independent judicial body which attempts to resolve employment disputes between employees and employers.

However, before the case is heard at an Employment Tribunal, the employee should inform the Advisory, Conciliation and Arbitration Service (ACAS), who will attempt to mediate a conciliation between the employee and employer.

If a settlement is not possible, tribunal proceedings can commence.

The remedies for unfair dismissal are wide-ranging and will be more advantageous to an employee than an action for wrongful dismissal.

The three remedies are:

Re-instatement	This is an order that the employee may return to the same job without any break in continuity. It will only be awarded if the applicant wishes it and if it is practicable.
Re-engagement	This is where an order is made to the effect that the employee must be given comparable employment. The EAT (Employment Appeal Tribunal) has ruled that a reengagement order will not be granted if there has been a breakdown of relationship and confidence between the two parties.
Compensation	This is the usual remedy in a case of unfair dismissal. There are three types of payment: the basic award, the compensatory award and the additional or special award. Basic award: This is based on the age of the employee and the number of years' continuous service Compensatory award: This award is given in addition to the basic award and compensates the employee for the loss suffered. For example, loss of wages and any other fringe benefits such as: access to a company car, commission on sales, potential retirement of redundancy benefits. Additional award: If the tribunal orders the employer to re-engage or re-instate the employee, the employer can refuse but the employer will have to pay additional compensation.

4.8 Redundancy

An employee is redundant if their dismissal is wholly or mainly attributable to the fact that:

- the employer has ceased, or intends to cease, business for the purposes for which the employee has been employed

- the employer has ceased, or intends to cease to carry on the business in the place where the employee was employed, or

- the requirements of that business for employees to carry out work of a particular kind, or for them to carry out the work in the place where they were so employed, have ceased or diminished.

Note that the work may have ceased altogether or only in the place where the employee was employed.

Redundancy consultation process

If employees and their representatives are not consulted, in a redundancy situation, the redundancy dismissals will almost certainly be unfair.

If an employer wishes to make 20 or more employees redundant in one place of work within a 90 day period, known as a collective redundancy situation, they must:

- Notify the Redundancy Payments Service; and
- Consult with workplace representatives. These may be either trade union representatives or, where no union is recognised, elected employee representatives instead. If employees choose not to elect employee representatives, relevant information must be communicated directly to each individual.

Consultation must start in good time – when redundancy proposals are in their formative stage – and at least:

- 30 days before the first redundancy where there are 20 to 99 proposed redundancies
- 45 days in advance where there are 100 or more proposed redundancies.

The following procedure will be followed:

The employee must have been continuously employed for two years

↓

The claim must go to the tribunal within six months of dismissal

↓

The employee must prove they were dismissed

↓

The employer must prove the employee is not redundant

↓

If found redundant, pay as per basic award for unfair dismissal.

Examples

Redundant employee: European Chefs Catering v Currell (1971)

A pastry cook was dismissed because the requirement for his specialty (éclairs and meringues) had ceased. He was replaced by a new pastry cook whose specialty was the new requirement (continental pastries).

HELD : It was held that the dismissed pastry cook had been dismissed for redundancy as the need for the particular work he contracted to do had ceased.

Not redundant: Vaux and Associated Breweries v Ward (1969)

A quiet public house was modernised by installing a discotheque. The 57 year old barmaid, Mrs Ward, was dismissed in order to make way for a younger more glamorous barmaid.

HELD: Mrs Ward had not been dismissed for redundancy as there was no change in the nature of the particular work being done.

The place where a person is employed means in this context the place where he is usually employed and any place where, under his contract, he can be required to work. There will not, therefore, be a redundancy situation where the transfer of location is reasonable or where the contract gives the employer the right to move the employee in question from one place to another. This is not the case, though, if the employer has no such right: O'Brien v Associated Fire Alarms (1969).

Redundancy pay

Redundancy pay is calculated in the same way as the basic award for unfair dismissal. Redundancy pay is dependent on the age of the employee:

Up to 22 years old   ½ week's pay for each year of service

22 up to 41 years old   1 week's pay for each year of service

41 years old plus   1 ½ week's pay for each year of service.

The maximum redundancy pay that can be paid is for 20 years of service.

However, an employee is not entitled to redundancy pay if they unreasonably refuse an offer of fresh employment (made before the old contract expires) to start within four weeks on the same or suitable terms. The employee must be allowed at least a four week trial period in the new job.

Whether the alternative employment offered is suitable, or the offer was unreasonably refused, are both questions of fact to be determined by reference to such matters as the employee's skill and working conditions, the requirements of his family, the location of a new role, a change in earnings, age, health, gender, etc.

Any dispute arising in this respect is for the tribunal to determine and the onus of proof is on the employer.

 Example

Taylor v Kent County Council (1969)

Taylor was the headmaster of a school. The school was amalgamated with another school and a new head appointed to the combined school. Taylor was offered employment in a pool of teachers, standing in for short periods in understaffed schools. He would retain his current salary.

HELD: Taylor was entitled to reject this offer and claim a redundancy payment: the new offer was substantially different, particularly in regard to status.

 Activity 10

Which of the following cannot justify the dismissal of an employee?

A   The employee's incompetence

B   The employee's misconduct

C   The employee's inability to do the job without breaking the law

D   That the employee intends to join an independent trade union

 Activity 11

Where a dismissed employee claims wrongful dismissal, which one of the following is incorrect?

A   The claim can be based on dismissal without prior notice

B   The claim can be brought to court, but not to tribunal

C   The claim will essentially be for breach of contract

D   The claimant does not need to resign immediately if seeking other employment

 Activity 12

Which remedy for unfair dismissal can be defined as: the employee must be given comparable employment but in a different position?

A   Re-instatement

B   Re-engagement

C   Compensation

Activity 13

Mike has worked continuously for Kappers Ltd for 15 years. What is the statutory minimum notice period his employer is required to give?

Tick the correct answer.

Statement	Correct?
A minimum of 15 weeks notice	
A maximum of 15 weeks notice	
A minimum of 12 weeks notice	
A maximum of 12 weeks notice	

 Activity 14

Janette started working for Kappers Ltd on 15th April 2016. It is now 20th March 2017.

What is the statutory minimum notice period her employer is required to give? Tick the most appropriate answer.

Statement	Correct?
None	
One week	
Two weeks	
One month	

 Activity 15

Ravi's job has been made redundant. Ravi is 25 years old and has worked for the same employer for 5 years. He earns £18,720 per annum.

Calculate the amount of redundancy pay Ravi is entitled to.

Activity 16

Gertrude, aged 61, had worked for Fabulous Fabrics for 25 years.

Which of the following best illustrates the calculation for the redundancy pay to which she will be entitled?

A   1.5 weeks' pay x 20

B   1.5 weeks' pay x 25

C   1 week's pay x 20

D   1 week's pay x 25

 Activity 17

Which of the following three statements regarding redundancy are true?

(i)   An employee can be deemed redundant if their dismissal is due to their employer deciding to move company operations to a different location

(ii)   If an employer wishes to make 20 or more employees redundant in one place of work within a 90 day period, they must notify the Redundancy Payments Service and consult with workplace representatives.

(iii)   Redundancy pay is the same regardless of the employee's age

Choose from the following options:

A   (i) and (ii) only

B   (ii) and (iii) only

C   (i) and (iii) only

D   (i), (ii) and (iii)

End of chapter activities

 Activity 18

Terms are implied into employment contracts under common law and statute. Which of the following is NOT a term implied by statute?

A   The employee has a right to a minimum level of pay

B   The employee has a right to not be unfairly dismissed

C   The employee has a right to four weeks paid leave each year

D   The employee has a right to be indemnified for necessary expenses

 Activity 19

The following statements relate to the employment status of a worker. Tick to show which statements are correct.

Statement	Correct?
An employee has a contract for service	
An employee receives statutory protection against unfair dismissal.	
Only employees can claim certain state benefits, such as statutory maternity pay.	

 Activity 20

An employee resigns due to a serious breach of her employment contract terms by her employer.

Which of the following remedies is open to the employee?

A   Redundancy pay

B   No remedy as she has resigned

C   Constructive dismissal

D   Statutory sick pay

Answers to chapter activities

 Activity 1

The correct answer is C.

As an independent contractor he would provide his own tools and pay income tax after payment. However, independent contractors would not be required to carry out the work personally and could send substitutes.

 Activity 2

The correct answer is C.

The other statements are all correct differences.

 Activity 3

The correct answer is A.

The control test is the one which would determine a worker's status.

 Activity 4

The correct answer is D.

Indira providing her own car for delivering cakes to offices suggests she is a contractor. Taken in isolation, the apron would not prove her to be employed, but is not an indication to the contrary.

 Activity 5

The correct answer is C.

Although employers should adhere to Equality Act 2010, this is a statutory duty not one implied by common law.

Activity 6

The correct answer is C.

An employee is entitled to a written statement of employment particulars within two months of commencing employment .

 Activity 7

The correct answer is B.

Formal qualifications would be included in a job specification rather than a contract of employment.

 Activity 8

The correct answer is A.

An employer does not need to supply references to all employees a reference, but those who require one should receive an honest reference.

 Activity 9

The correct answer is D.

An employee only has a duty to obey orders given to them by the employer if they are reasonable and lawful.

 Activity 10

The correct answer is D.

Dismissal based on the employee's trade union membership would be considered unfair.

 Activity 11

The correct answer is B.

Where a dismissed employee claims wrongful dismissal, the claim can be brought to a tribunal.

Activity 12

The correct answer is B.

Re-instatement is where the employee must be given comparable employment but in a different position.

 Activity 13

Statement	Correct?
A minimum of 15 weeks notice	
A maximum of 15 weeks notice	
A minimum of 12 weeks notice	✓
A maximum of 12 weeks notice	

 Activity 14

Statement	Correct?
None (Janette has been employed for less than two years)	✓
One week	
Two weeks	
One month	

 Activity 15

2 years @ ½ week: £180 x 2 = £360.

3 years @ 1 week: £360 x 3 = £1,080.

Therefore the answer is **£1,440.**

Activity 16

The correct answer is A.

Gertrude is entitled to 1.5 week's pay for each year of service over the age of 41 to a maximum of 20 years.

 Activity 17

The correct answer is A.

Both (i) and (ii) are true, but the age of the employee is considered when calculating either redundancy pay or unfair dismissal compensation.

 Activity 18

The correct answer is D.

The employee's right to be indemnified for necessary expenses results from common law.

Activity 19

Statement	Correct?
An employee has a contract for service	
An employee receives statutory protection against unfair dismissal.	✓
Only employees can claim certain state benefits, such as statutory maternity pay.	✓

 Activity 20

The correct answer is C.

Constructive dismissal would be the remedy sought.

Company Law

Introduction

In this chapter, we will address all of the key components of company law. In doing so, we will explain the differences between different types of business structure and you will learn about the implications of setting up a new company and be able to contrast this with the alternatives of operating either as a sole trader or in a partnership.

ASSESSMENT CRITERIA	CONTENTS
4.1 Identify differences between companies, sole traders and partnerships	1 Business structure
	2 Company formation
	3 Company information
4.2 Identify issues to be considered when forming a company	4 Legislative requirements for companies
4.3 Identify the books, records, accounts and returns that a company must keep or file	

1 Business structure

1.1 Types of business structure

There are several types of structures which can be used to operate a business.

The type of structure used will determine the amount of tax paid, the amount of paperwork that is legally required, and the personal liability faced by the owners of the business.

For the purposes of this unit, we will firstly discuss four common structures for start-up businesses:

- Sole trader
- Partnership
- Limited company (Ltd)
- Limited liability partnership (LLP)

1.2 Sole traders

A sole trader is the simplest form of business structure.

Key attributes of a sole trader include:

- The business is owned by one person who provides capital investment and has total control;
- The owner is entitled to all profits earned by the business;
- The owner is personally responsible for all debts of the business and has **unlimited liability;**
- The owner is personally liable for income tax;
- The owner can sue or can be sued for breach of contract; negligence, etc.
- There are no legal requirements to publish financial statements, although HMRC will need to see at least a basic set of accounts for tax purposes.

In this type of business structure, the owner and the business are one and the same. i.e. the owner is the **legal entity**. Although sole trader organisations can be large enough to employ several people to help operate the business, it can be difficult for the business to grow beyond a certain size through lack of expertise.

Sole traders can use a 'business name', however the name of the business owner must be stated on all business documentation. This is because the business is not a separate legal entity and in the event of a breach of contract or negligence, it will be the owner who will be personally liable.

1.3 Partnerships

A partnership is the simplest form of combined ownership. The owners can share their expertise to expand the business.

Key attributes of partnerships include:

- The business is owned by two or more persons who between them provide the capital Investment and control the business.

- Each partner is an agent for the partnership, e.g. each party can commit the business to contracts

- No formal agreement is legally required although it is recommended that a Partnership Agreement is drawn up to agree how profits from the business are shared (in the absence of a Partnership Agreement, the Partnership Act of 1890 applies – a 50:50 split between partners)

- Each partner is 'jointly and severally' liable for all the debts of the partnership. In the event of one partner being unable to pay their share of the debt, the other partners will be liable. Likewise, a claimant can choose which partner to sue if not suing both (e.g. if one partner was rich and the other was poor).

- Each partner is personally liable for income tax

- There are no legal requirements to publish financial statements, although specific accounting records must be maintained.

Definition

A legal entity is a company, partnership or individual which has the legal capacity to:

- enter into agreements or contracts
- assume obligations
- incur and pay debts
- sue and be sued in its own right
- be accountable for illegal activities

It can be seen that both sole traders and partnerships share common characteristics. In particular, in both cases it is the individual owners of the business who are personally liable for the debts of the business (**unlimited liability**) and the businesses **is not** a separate **legal entity.**

Example

Charles and Elaine form a partnership called CE Foods that delivers lunch-time snacks from the back of a van. Due to a power failure back at their headquarters some of the food has been contaminated.

As a result, their customers suffered food poisoning.

As a partnership both Charles and Elaine are liable. All of their possessions (including their homes) could be required to be sold to pay damages.

To protect themselves from this happening, most sole traders and partnerships take out insurance cover.

Some of the drawbacks of being held personally liable can be overcome by the creation of a company.

1.4   Companies

There are many reasons for forming a company, especially when a business interest shows growth.

 Definition

Incorporation is the legal process used to form a company and results in the company being recognised as having a legal personality separate and distinct from its human members.

There are two options when forming a company, as shown below:

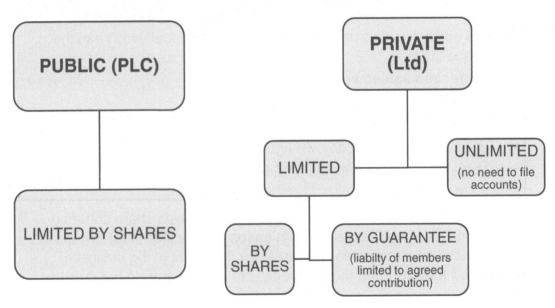

KAPLAN PUBLISHING

1.5   Private Limited Companies (Ltd)

A private limited company is a business that is owned by its shareholders (who invest in the company to provide it with the capital (money) to operate), run by directors and, **most importantly,** where the liability of shareholders for the debts of the company is limited.

The main advantage of a company structure is that it provides the owners of the business with a right to participate in the profits without any personal liability (the company absorbs the entire liability of the business).

For private limited companies:

- The company is a separate **legal entity.** The company, not the owners, can make contracts, incur debts, and can sue and be sued in its own right.

- Owners are shareholders in the company. They are entitled to a share of any distributions (dividends) made from the company's profit and to a share of any residual assets when the company is wound up.

- The day-to-day running of the company is managed by **directors** who have a responsibility to the shareholders to :

    o ensure long-term sustainability

    o establish policies aimed at maximising shareholder wealth, and

    o to safeguard the assets in the limited company.

  Company directors aren't personally responsible for debts the business can't pay if it goes wrong, as long as they haven't broken the law.

- Most limited companies are 'limited by shares'. This means that the shareholders' responsibilities for the company's financial liabilities are limited to the value of shares that they own but haven't paid for. Therefore, the shareholders have **limited liability.**

- The company is liable to pay Corporation Tax instead of Income Tax.

1.6 Advantages and disadvantages of forming a company

The key advantages and disadvantages of forming a company with a separate legal entity are shown in the table below:

Advantages	Disadvantages
Each shareholder is liable to contribute only the amount owing for shares held	Administration – a considerable amount of documentation is required
Perpetual ownership	Lack of privacy - accounts and business details are available to the general public
Company owns its own assets	Greater business expenses (e.g. registrar's fees, auditors)
Company may sue and be sued	Restrictions and bureaucracy - subject to technical rules and regulations
Ease of borrowing (against assets)	

Example

Pablo decides he is going to form a company with his friend Marvin. They decide to issue 100 shares valued at £1 each when it is set up and split the company 60:40.

Pablo takes 60 shares and pays £60. Marvin takes 40 shares but only pays £20, owing the company £20 for the remainder.

If the company goes bust, Marvin must pay £20 to cover his unpaid shares. Pablo is not required to pay anything.

1.7 Public Limited Companies (plc)

Shares in private limited companies cannot be offered for sale to the general public, so the availability of finance is restricted, especially if the business wants to expand.

Therefore, it may be attractive to change status to a public limited company (plc) so that it is **able to offer its shares to the public**.

The shares of public companies may be traded on a recognised stock exchange, although they do not have to be.

The main advantages of being a plc are:

- **better access to capital** – i.e. raising share capital from existing and new investors. Investors are more likely to invest in a public company because there is less risk and more potential to reap large rewards.

- to give a company a more **prestigious profile**

Some disadvantages to being a plc (as opposed to remaining as a Ltd company) are:

- the company is likely to have a much larger number of external shareholders to whom company directors will be accountable

- greater public scrutiny of the company's financial performance and actions. Public companies must comply with the rules established by the Sarbanes-Oxley Act, which was enacted to protect investors.

1.8 Private company versus public company

The following table summarises the basic differences between public and private limited companies:

	Public companies	**Private (limited) companies**
Name	Ends with plc or public limited company.	Ends with Ltd or Limited.
Capital	Must have allotted shares of at least the "authorised maximum" value of £50,000.	No minimum or maximum requirements.
Raising capital	May raise capital by advertising its shares as available for public subscription.	Prohibited from offering its shares to the public.
Start of trading	Must obtain trading certificate from registrar before they can start trading.	Can begin from the date of incorporation.
Directors	Minimum of two.	Minimum of one.
Company secretary	Must have one. Must be qualified.	Does not need to have one.
Accounts	Must file accounts within 6 months.	Must file accounts within 9 months.
Audit	Accounts must be audited.	Audit is not required where turnover is less than £6.5m.
Annual General Meeting	Must be held each year.	Need not hold an AGM.

1.9 Limited Liability Partnerships (LLP)

A Limited Liability Partnership is a cross between a Company and a Partnership.

The LLP structure is commonly used by accountants to retain the tax structure of traditional partnerships whilst adding some limited liability protection. LLPs are also becoming more common among firms in the legal profession such as solicitors.

LLPs are governed by the **Limited Liability Partnerships Act 2000**. A UK limited liability partnership is a corporate body – i.e. it is a separate **legal entity**.

Key factors:

- The business is owned by two or more persons (partners) who between them provide capital Investment and control the business.

- Each partner is an agent for the partnership, e.g. each party can commit the business to contracts

- Profits from the business are distributed to the partners as self-employed persons who are each liable for income tax.

- Each partner is liable for a share of the debts of the partnership as set out in an LLP agreement but are not 'severally' responsible for the other partners. Partners cannot lose more than what they have invested.

- There are no legal requirements to publish financial statements, although specific accounting records must be maintained.

KAPLAN PUBLISHING

2 Company formation

2.1 The process of setting up a limited company

There are more than three million limited companies registered in the UK, with hundreds of thousands of new companies incorporated each year.

To set up a limited company there are a number of documents to be submitted to the Registrar of Companies at Companies House under the Companies Act 2006.

Companies can be registered online or by post using form IN01 from HMRC.

 Definition

Companies House is the government body which incorporates and dissolves limited companies, registers and stores the information companies are legally required to supply, and makes this information available to the general public in the official government register of UK companies.

The website for more information is:
https://www.gov.uk/government/organisations/companies-house

By registering with Companies House, companies make their details public. Some information can be obtained from Companies House for free, including:

- company information (e.g. registered address, date of incorporation)
- current and resigned officers
- document images
- mortgage charge data
- previous company names
- insolvency information
- company accounts

For a small charge other filed documents can be obtained, e.g. annual reports, annual returns and confirmation statements.

To register a limited company, the following information is required:

- **Application Form (IN01)** which gives details about the:
    - **proposed company name** (see section below: 'What's in a name?')
    - **registered office address** for the company where official communications will be sent
    - **main type of business activity** of the company by standard industry classification (SIC) code (e.g. event catering activities, solicitors, satellite communications activities)
- **Articles of Association** – these are the written rules about how the company is run. For example, they will give details of the level of authority held by the director(s) and who should attend meetings. These rules will also state how dividends (payments to shareholders) will be paid. If these articles are not supplied, **the model articles** (a set of default company rules) will apply if they are not supplied
- **Statement of Proposed Officers** who will be legally responsible for running the company and making sure company accounts and reports are completed properly. This includes:
    - **the name of at least one director** for private companies (two are required for public companies),
    - **the name of the company secretary** (it is not mandatory for private companies to list a company secretary but public companies must have one)
- **Statement of capital** which includes the number and monetary value of shares held by each shareholders, and the names and addresses of those shareholders. Each shareholder will receive a share of any profit the company makes, paid out in the form of dividends. The statement of capital also includes what share of dividends each shareholder will receive and whether they can vote on certain company matters.
- **Memorandum of Association** – this is a legal statement signed by all of the initial shareholders ('subscribers') that they agree to form the company.

Example

What's in a name?

The name of any organisation (including sole traders and partnerships) must be unique cannot be the 'same as', or 'too like' another registered company's name.

'Same as' names are those where the only difference to an existing name is:

- punctuation
- a special character, for example a + or ! sign

For example, 'Hands UK Ltd' and 'Hand's Ltd' are the same as 'Hands Ltd' and 'Box.com Ltd' is the same as 'Box Ltd'.

'Too like' names may need to be changed if someone complains and Companies House agrees it is too similar a name previously registered, as this can be misleading and cause confusion.

For example, 'Dynamic Technology LLP' is too like 'Dinamix Technology LLP'.

Company names also cannot:

- contain a sensitive word or expression unless you get permission
- suggest a connection with the government, official bodies or the local authorities
- be offensive

Company names can be changed after incorporation according to the rules set out in the company's articles of association. For example, the rule may specify that any name change would require 75% approval by the members.

 Activity 1

Which of the following is incorrect in relation to company names?

A   In general, the name of a private or public company must end in 'limited', 'Ltd', 'public limited company' or 'plc' as appropriate

B   The name must not be the same as that of an existing company

C   The name cannot be changed without the unanimous approval of the shareholders

Activity 2

Which of the following names could not without further consent be a permissible name under the Companies Act for a company, the main object of which is refuse collection services for Westminster City Council?

A   Westminster City Refuse Services Ltd.

B   Council (Refuse Collection) Services Ltd.

C   Refuse Collection (Westminster) Ltd.

D   City Waste Disposal Ltd.

 Activity 3

Which of the following documents need to be supplied in order to register a limited company? Tick all that apply.

A memorandum of association	
A letter on headed notepaper	
A company tax return	
A statement of capital	

2.2   Displaying the name of the company

Regulations made under the Companies Act 2006 require a company to display its name at its registered office and other places of business, on business documents and on websites.

The purpose of the regulations is that the legal identity of every company should be revealed to anyone who have, or may wish to have, dealings with it.

Legally, the following must contain company details:

Company signage	Every company must display a sign with its registered name at any location at which it carries on business. The signs need to be: • in characters that can be read with the naked eye • displayed in such a way that visitors to that office, place or location may easily see it continuously.
Business stationery	The company's registered name must be shown in all forms of business correspondence and documentation, whether in hard copy or electronic, for example: • business letters, notices and other official publications • business emails • order forms • written orders for goods or services to be supplied to the business • invoices, delivery notes and receipts issued in the course of the business • written demands for payment of debts arising in the course of the business • cheques signed on behalf of the company.
Websites	Every company must disclose its registered name on its websites. The company name does not have to be on every page but it must be visible and easily read.

In addition to the registered company name, on business stationery (letters, order forms, etc.) and websites, companies must show:

• the company's registered number (as provided by Companies House)

• its registered office address

• where the company is registered (England and Wales, Scotland or Northern Ireland)

• the fact that it's a limited company (usually by spelling out the company's full name including 'Limited' or 'Ltd')

Sole traders or partnerships who use a different trading name, must display their own name (sole trader) or all the partners' names (partnership) in a prominent position at all their business premises.

Activity 4

Where must a company's name be displayed?

Tick ALL that apply.

On invoices they issue to customers	
On signage at their business premises	
On a noticeboard at the local council offices	
On business letters and e-mails	

Activity 5

Which of the following information must companies show on all company documents, publicity and letters in order to comply with Companies Act 2006?

Tick ALL that apply.

Registered office address	
Directors' addresses	
Company's telephone number	
Company's registration number	

2.3   Certificate of Incorporation

The Certificate of Incorporation is issued by Companies House as conclusive evidence that the registration requirements of the Companies Act 2006 have been complied with and that the company is duly registered under this Act. The certificate will state:

- the name and registered number of the company;
- the date of its incorporation;
- that the company type is private limited by shares;
- whether the company's registered office is situated in England, Wales, Scotland or in Northern Ireland.

The certificate will be authenticated by the registrar's official seal.

THE COMPANIES ACT 2006

Company No. **7361045**

The Registrar of Companies for England and Wales hereby certifies that

IL PRINCIPE LTD

was incorporated under the **Companies Act 2006**

as a private company on the **31st August 2010**, that the company is **limited by shares** and the situation of its registered office is in **England/Wales**.

Given at Companies House, the **12th November 2013**

R J DAVIES
for the Registrar of Companies

Companies House

Activity 6

There are a number of important legal differences between an incorporated business (company) and an unincorporated business (e.g. a partnership).

Which of the following are characteristics of a company? Tick all that apply.

Companies are created by a formal registration procedure	
A company is subject to the requirements of the Companies Act 2006	
There is no separation of ownership and management in a company	
Companies must legally disclose certain financial information to the general public	
Directors in a company are personally liable for the debts of the business	

 Activity 7

All of the following statements about the formation of a company in the United Kingdom are true except one.

Which of the following is incorrect?

A   The company comes into existence when the Registrar of Companies issues a Certificate of Incorporation

B   The company comes into existence when granted a listing by the Stock Exchange.

C   A company can have just one member.

D   A public company must have a certificate of incorporation and a trading certificate before it can commence business.

2.4   Registering for Corporation Tax

In addition to registering the company with Companies House, it also needs to be registered with HMRC for Corporation Tax purposes.

This must be done within three months of starting to do business. In this sense, 'doing business' includes buying, selling, employing someone, advertising, renting a property or certain other activities.

Companies may have to pay a penalty if they register late.

2.5   Who pays Corporation Tax?

All UK limited companies are subject to Corporation Tax. The tax is charged as a percentage of the annual profits made by a company.

Corporation Tax is not paid by businesses operating as sole traders or general and limited liability partnerships. The individuals running such businesses are classed as self-employed and will pay income tax on their business profits through the annual self- assessment system.

Corporation Tax does apply to the following organisations, even if they are not incorporated:

- Members' clubs, societies and associations
- Trade associations
- Housing associations
- Groups of individuals carrying on a business but not as a partnership, (for example, co-operatives.)

Sole traders and partnerships must also register with HMRC as soon as possible after starting the business. Registration should happen no later than 5th October in the second tax year of the business. Registration includes registering for self-assessment tax returns and the appropriate class of National Insurance contributions.

 Example

John started a business in May 2015 so he will need to register with HMRC by 5th October 2016 at the very latest.

Sole traders pay income tax and capital gains tax on the profit from the business. Each partner pays his own income tax and capital gains tax on his share of the partnership's profits and gains.

2.6   Limited Liability Partnerships (LLPs)

An LLP must be registered with Companies House, however LLPs are not subject to Corporation Tax.

To set up a limited liability partnership there are a number of documents to be prepared and regulations to follow under the Limited Liability Partnerships Act 2000. These include:

- Appointing two 'designated members' who have more responsibilities than ordinary members, e.g. keeping company accounts.
- Drawing up a limited liability partnership (LLP) agreement. This document sets out how the LLP will be run, including:
  - how profits are shared among members
  - who needs to agree decisions

- members' responsibilities
- how members can join or leave the LLP
- Giving notice to Companies House of any changes
- Preparing and submitting a confirmation statement (annual return) of the Ltd. Company to Companies House
- Filing annual accounts of the Limited Liability Partnership
- Notifying Companies House of the appointment of a corporate secretary and any subsequent changes to their details in the Limited Liability Company

2.7 Lifting the corporate veil

Limited Liability Companies exist in part to shield the personal assets of shareholders from personal liability for the debts or actions of a corporation.

 Definition

Lifting the corporate veil is when the courts look through the company records to find the identity of the shareholders.

The courts will lift the corporate veil to prevent owners making unfair use of a legal technicality. The corporate veil has been lifted both by statutory measures and common law cases.

Examples

Statutory examples of where the corporate veil may be lifted

Legislation	Action
Companies Act 2006	There may be potential to avoid taxation by moving assets/liabilities around a group of related companies. S399 of Companies Act 2006 requires group accounts to be prepared which recognise the common link between them.
Insolvency Act 1986	Members and/or directors may be personally liable for wrongful or fraudulent trading. For example, continuing to trade when it is obvious that the company is insolvent and cannot pay its bills.
Company Director's Disqualification Act 1986	A disqualified person will be jointly or severally liable if they take part in the promotion, formation or management of any company.

Common Law examples of where the corporate veil may be lifted

Sham companies	**Gilford Motor Co Ltd v Horne 1933** A former employee was bound by a promise in his contract of employment not to solicit customers from his former employer. He set up a company to do just that. **HELD:** The court found the company (and the corporate personality) a front for Mr Horne and issued an injunction to prevent him from continuing.
Nationality	In times of war it is illegal to trade with the enemy. It may be possible to lift the corporate veil. **Daimler Co Ltd v Continental Tyre & Rubber 1916** Continental Tyre & Rubber was incorporated in England but all the directors except one were German. During the Great War, Daimler Co Ltd refused to pay an unpaid debt to Continental Tyre & Rubber claiming the company was an alien enemy. **HELD:** The court decided this was a matter of national emergency and that the corporate veil could be lifted. Daimler Co Ltd did not have to pay Continental Tyre & Rubber as to do so would be to trade with the enemy.
Family investment	**Prest v Petrodel Resources Ltd 2013** There were a number of properties owned by the Petrodel Group, a group of companies wholly owned by a husband. The issue was whether the corporate veil could be lifted so that the wife could seek financial relief from the properties owned by these companies. **HELD:** The properties had been funded by the husband's money rather than that of the Petrodel Group companies. As the husband was a beneficial owner of the properties they were deemed to form part of his estate and the wife would have financial recourse to the properties following divorce. However, the significance of *Prest* v Petrodel was that it suggested that piercing the veil was usually a last resort.

2.8   Off the shelf companies

Rather than forming a new company themselves, those wishing to set up a company may buy one 'ready-made' or 'off the shelf' from a company formation dealer.

The dealer will hold in stock a number of ready-made companies with generally non-descriptive names (e.g. Newco123). The company can either trade with an existing name, or have the existing name changed to one of the purchaser's choice, subject to availability.

Buying off the shelf has a number of advantages as follows:

*   cheap and simple (no need to pay for accountants or solicitors separately)
*   can trade immediately
*   no problem of pre-incorporation contracts.

2.9   Pre-incorporation contracts

 Definition

A **pre-incorporation contract** is where a person enters into a contract before a company has been registered.

The position at common law is that a company, prior to its incorporation, does not have contractual capacity and after its formation it cannot ratify or formally adopt a pre-incorporation contract. The promoter (the person undertaking to form the company) is therefore personally liable under any such contract. This is because a company does not legally exist until it is incorporated.

 Example

Kelner v Baxter (1866)

A, B and C entered into a contract with the claimant to purchase goods on behalf of the proposed Gravesend Royal Alexandra Hotel Co. The goods were supplied and used in the business. Shortly after incorporation the company collapsed.

HELD: As the Gravesend Royal Alexandra Hotel Co was not in existence when the contract was made it was not bound by the contract and could not be sued for the price of the goods. Neither could it ratify the contract after incorporation.

Activity 8

A business has been registered under the name 'The Mark Jones Partnership Co Ltd'. What type of business organisation must this be?

A   A partnership

B   A private limited company

C   A public limited company

D   Any of the above as this is a business name

Activity 9

Which of the following is NOT a legal requirement of a public company?

A   Name must end with 'plc' or 'public limited company'

B   Must have a minimum of two directors

C   Must have a company secretary

D   Must file accounts within 9 months.

Activity 10

The following statements relate to the shares of companies whose names end in 'Ltd'.

Tick all which are correct statements.

The shares may not be offered to the public.	
The shares may not be traded on the stock exchange.	
The allocation of shares cannot be changed.	
The company must start with shares worth £100 each.	

Activity 11

Complete the paragraph below using the pick list provided.

In a general partnership the partners are _____ liable for the debts of the company. In contrast when business is carried on through a company _____ by shares, the_____ is fully liable for any debts contracted rather than the shareholders.

A company is a separate _____ at law and if the shareholders have fully paid the amount due on their _____ they cannot be called upon to make any further contribution. The rules governing the relationship between the company and its shareholders is set down in the company's _____.

Pick list

directors   Articles of Association   Memorandum of Association

company   person   shares   jointly   not at all   public   limited

Activity 12

In company law, in which of the following circumstances has it been seen as necessary to 'lift the corporate veil'? Tick all that apply.

Where a company is sham, established to help avoid contractual obligations	
To identify the true nationality of a company	
To establish if a disqualified director is participating in the management of a company	

Activity 13

Which of the following statements is correct?

(i) Purchasing an 'off the shelf' company enables a business to commence more quickly

(ii) It is generally cheaper to purchase an 'off the shelf' company than to arrange for a solicitor or accountant to register a new company

(iii) The creation of a Public Limited Company can enable both greater prestige for the company and better access to capital.

Choose from the list below:

A (i) and (ii) only

B (ii) and (iii) only

C (i) and (iii) only

D (i), (ii) and (iii)

Activity 14

Viola and Victor decided to form a company.

On 1 March 20X6, they sent the necessary documents to the registrar. On 10 May 20X6, they received the certificate of incorporation dated 1 May 20X6. Subsequently they discovered that the company was registered on 1 June 20X6.

What was the date of incorporation?

A 1 March 20X6

B 1 May 20X6

C 10 May 20X6

D 1 June 20X6

Activity 15

Indicate whether the following statements are true or false:

Statement	True/False
It is not possible to register a company limited by shares with the same name as a company already on the register.	
Once on the register, a company limited by shares cannot change its registered office.	
The articles of association form the agreement of all initial shareholders to create a company.	
The articles of association of a company limited by shares contain the internal regulations of the company.	

 Activity 16

Tina and Kirstie have carried on business together in partnership for a number of years. They have now decided to operate their business through the medium of a private company limited by shares called Tink & Corn Ltd.

Complete the following sentences:

As partners, the liability of Tina and Kirstie for the firm's debts was (individual / joint / nothing).

In order to register a private company limited by shares the partners will need to submit a number of documents to the Registrar of Companies. These include (a statement of capital / a statement of intent) and an application form including (the proposed name of the company / the company business plan and financial projections) and (details of the directors' history / details of the registered office).

If the registrar of Companies is satisfied with the documents, he will issue a (Certificate / Memorandum / Statement) of Incorporation which enables the company to commence trading (immediately / after a week / after three months).

If the company becomes insolvent, Tina and Kirstie will be liable (for all of the company debt / for none of the company debt / for any unpaid portion of the price of their shares).

3 Company information

3.1 Requirements of limited companies

Once registered, a limited company must keep or file (submit to Companies House) books, records, accounts and returns.

> ### 🔍 Definition
>
> In this context to file is the legal definition for delivering a document to a government body as an official record.

This includes the following:

- Confirmation Statement
- Statutory Books
- Annual Accounts
- Company Tax Return

3.2 Confirmation Statement

UK Company Law requires every limited company and limited liability partnership (LLP) to submit a Confirmation Statement (previously known as an Annual Return) to Companies House **every year**. The Confirmation Statement is used to check the information on the Companies House register is correct, including:

- the details of the registered office, directors, secretary and the registered address
- the information on the statement of capital and shareholder information
- the standard industry classification (SIC code]

3.3 Statutory Books

The company must also keep accurate and up to date records of the following at the company's registered address:

- the names of the directors, shareholders and company secretaries
- the results of any shareholder votes and resolutions made in meetings
- promises the company makes for payments if something goes wrong and it's the company's fault ('indemnities')
- transactions when someone buys shares in the company

- loans or mortgages secured against the company's assets

3.4   Accounting records which must be kept

Limited companies are required by law to keep accounting records.
Failure to do so will result in a fine by HMRC and could result in company
directors being disqualified.   Although organisations which are not
registered as limited companies, e.g. sole traders and partnerships are not
required to keep detailed records it is recommended that they do so for
HMRC purposes.

Transactions	Books	Records
All money received and spent by the company	Cash Receipts book Cash Payments book Petty Cash book	Bank statements Credit card statements Cheque stubs Petty Cash vouchers Receipts Till rolls
Details of assets owned by the company	Fixed Asset Register	Purchase invoices
Debts the company owes or is owed	Subsidiary Purchases Ledger Subsidiary Sales Ledger	Purchase and Sales invoices Customer and Supplier Statements
Inventory held by the company at the end of the financial year		Stock listing Purchase invoices [for costs]
All goods bought and sold	Sales and sales returns day books Purchase and purchase day books Cash books	Sales and purchase **orders** Sales and purchase **delivery notes** Sales and purchase **invoices** Cash **receipts** Till rolls

3.5   How long to keep records

Records must normally be kept for at least 6 years from the end of the last
company financial year they relate to.

3.6 Annual accounts (Financial statements)

After the end of its financial year, private limited companies must prepare and file

- full 'statutory' or annual accounts, and
- a Company Tax Return

Statutory (or annual) accounts include a set of financial statements;

- a **statement of financial position**, which shows the value of everything the company owns, owes and is owed on the last day of the financial year
- a **statement of profit and loss**, which shows the company's sales, running costs and the profit or loss it has made over the financial year
- notes about the accounts, which give further explanation, for example stock valuation and depreciation methods used.
- a director's report, which confirms that the accounts filed are a true and fair reflection of the business.

The statutory accounts must meet either:

- International Financial Reporting Standards (IFRS)
- UK Generally Accepted Accounting Practice (GAAP)

Both of these are designed to ensure consistent approaches and regulation to the preparation of company accounts.

3.7 Company Tax Return

Corporation Tax is charged on the profits made by a company for a specific period.

The company tax return will show profit or loss for Corporation Tax purposes and the amount of Corporation Tax to be paid.

A tax return still needs to be filed even if there is no tax due.

The following filing dates and payment deadlines currently apply:

Action	Deadline
File first accounts with Companies House	21 months after the date you registered with Companies House
File annual accounts with Companies House	9 months after your company's financial year ends
Pay Corporation Tax or tell HMRC that your limited company does not owe any	9 months and 1 day after your 'accounting period' for Corporation Tax ends
File a Company Tax Return	12 months after your 'accounting period' for Corporation Tax ends

Activity 17

Within what period of time after the 'accounting period' must a private limited company file its accounts?

A   Six months

B   Nine months

C   Twelve months

D   Whenever it is ready

 Activity 18

Which of the following does a limited company need to file:

(i)   Company Tax Return

(ii)   Confirmation Statement

(iii) Statutory accounts including a Statement of Financial Position

Choose one of the following options:

A   (i) and (ii) only

B   (ii) and (iii) only

C   (i) and (iii) only

D   (i), (ii) and (iii)

 Activity 19

Which of the following accounting records must companies keep to comply with Companies Act 2006?

Tick ALL that apply.

	✓
Details of income	
Details of expenditure	
Details of assets owned by the company	
Details of liabilities owed by the company	
Details of money spent by the company	
Details of money received by the company	

4 Legislative requirements for businesses

4.1 Introduction

Having recognised the importance of legal contracts, both for employees and customers, we have also seen how legislation can influence the daily operations of any business. In the workplace, you will encounter numerous regulations resulting from Acts of Parliament.

Some of these Acts of Parliament have been addressed previously – for example, the impact of Sale of Goods Act 1979 on consumer rights (also the Consumer Rights Act 2015) and the role of Equality Act 2010 in reducing discrimination in all aspects of employment.

We will now look at two further areas where legislation must be considered in business: health and safety and data protection.

4.2 Health and Safety at Work etc Act 1974

There are many potential hazards in any workplace. To address these threats, detailed legislation has been passed to regulate working conditions. The **Health and Safety at Work etc Act 1974** (also referred to as HSWA, the HSW Act, the 1974 Act or HASAWA) is the main piece of legislation covering health and safety in the workplace in the UK. The Act places a duty on employers "to ensure, so far as is reasonably practicable, the health, safety and welfare at work" of all their employees.

The Health and Safety Executive (HSE), working alongside local authorities, is responsible for enforcing the Act and a number of other Acts and Statutory Instruments relevant to the working environment.

The Act requires that employers ensure:

- safe operation and maintenance of the working environment, plant and systems
- maintenance of safe access and egress to the workplace
- safe use, handling and storage of dangerous substances
- adequate training of staff to ensure health and safety
- adequate welfare provisions for staff at work.

Employers are also required to maintain a written record of health and safety policy and consult with employees or their representatives on such policies (should they employ five or more workers).

4.3 Further Health and Safety Regulations

The **Management of Health and Safety at Work Regulations 1999** places a duty on employers to assess and manage risks to their employees and others arising from work activities.

Employers must also make arrangements for emergencies, offer adequate information and training for employees, and provide health surveillance where appropriate.

The **Workplace (Health, Safety and Welfare) Regulations 1992** are concerned with making the working environment safe and suitable for employees and cover varied aspects, including office ventilation, lighting, temperature, room dimensions, seating arrangements, washing facilities, provision of drinking water, rest and break facilities.

In addition to the Workplace (Health, Safety and Welfare) Regulations there are the **Health and Safety (Display Screen Equipment) Regulations**, which relate directly to use of display screen equipment (DSE). In general these are in place to ensure that workstations and jobs are well designed for individuals, and that the risks to health and safety are minimised.

In all cases, these laws are regulations. As previously explained, this means that they are all derived from EU law.

4.4 Data Protection Act 1998

In the modern world, health and safety is not the only area where legislation is deemed necessary to protect individuals in the workplace. As the business world becomes more complex, organisations are holding increasing amounts of data about individuals.

Data protection is concerned with protecting individuals against the misuse of this information.

The **1998 Data Protection Act** covers how information about living **identifiable** persons is processed and used. It is much broader in scope than the earlier 1984 Act, in that ALL organisations that hold or process personal data MUST comply. This Act has implications for everyone who processes manual or electronic personal data. It applies to filing systems of records held on computer or manual sets of accessible records e.g. a database of customer names, addresses, telephone numbers and sales details.

The Data Protection Act stipulates that personal data is kept securely and that it should be accurate. Under the terms of the Act, the need for privacy is recognised by the requirements that all data should be held for clearly designated purposes. Accuracy and integrity must be maintained and data must be open to inspection. Only legitimate parties can access data and information must be secured against alteration, accidental loss or deliberate damage. Furthermore, the Act states that data must be obtained fairly, to precise specifications and must not be kept for longer than required.

It reinforces the need for confidentiality in business dealings. A business should not reveal information about one customer to another or information about its employees without their permission. The Act gives a data subject, with some exceptions, the right to examine the personal data that a data controller is holding about him or her. Where personal data is being held, the subject has the right to receive details of:

(i)   the personal data that is being held about them

(ii)   the purposes for which this information is being processed

(iii)   the recipients to whom the information might be disclosed.

The data subject is also entitled to receive this information in a form that can be understood. In practice, this usually means providing the data subject with a printout of the data, and an explanation of any items of data (such as codes) whose meaning is not clear.

Any individual who suffers damage as a result of improper use of the data by the data controller is entitled to compensation for any loss suffered.

Also relating to information security, the **Computer Misuse Act 1990** makes it a criminal offence to attempt to access, use or alter any computer data, program or service to which you have not been granted authorised access rights. Therefore any attempt to interfere with or bypass the security controls, to attempt to obtain information such as other people's passwords, or accessing or modifying other people's programs or files without permission are offences under the Act. Amongst other things, this Act makes the activity of hacking illegal as well as the introduction of viruses and worms.

 Activity 20

Which of the following pieces of legislation is concerned with the misuse of information?

A   Sale of Goods Act 1979

B   Data Protection Act 1998

C   Equality Act 2010

D   Health and Safety at Work etc 1974

End of chapter activities

 Activity 21

Which of the following statements regarding limited companies is correct?

A   Public limited companies have access to a wider pool of finance than partnerships or sole traders.

B   Both public and private limited companies are allowed to sell shares to the public.

C   Companies are always owned by many different investors.

D   Shareholders are liable for any debts the company may incur.

 Activity 22

Which ONE of the following statements is true?

A   Partnerships offer the same benefits to investors as limited companies.

B   Sole traders have no personal liability for business debts.

C   Limited companies are classed as a separate legal entity; therefore the shareholders are not personally liable for any debts of the business.

D   A partnership can be made up of no more than 20 partners.

 Activity 23

Public limited companies are subject to tighter rules regarding the directors' dealings with the company, must hold an Annual General Meeting and also are required to have a Company Secretary. None of which do strictly speaking apply to private companies.

Is this statement true or false?

Answers to chapter activities

 ### Activity 1

The correct answer is C.

This is incorrect as the name can be changed should the shareholders pass a resolution to do so, in accordance with the Articles of Association (e.g. with at least 75% voting in favour at a meeting).

 ### Activity 2

The correct answer is B.

The use of the word 'Council' in the business name would not be permitted.

Activity 3

A memorandum of association	✓
A letter on headed notepaper	
A company tax return	
A statement of capital	✓

Activity 4

On invoices they issue to customers	✓
On signage at their business premises	✓
On a noticeboard at the local council offices	
On business letters and e-mails	✓

Activity 5

Registered office address	✓
Directors' addresses	
Company's telephone number	
Company's registration number	✓

Activity 6

Companies are created by a formal registration procedure	✓
A company is subject to the requirements of the Companies Act 2006	✓
There is no separation of ownership and management in a company	
Companies must legally disclose certain financial information to the general public	✓
Directors in a company are personally liable for the debts of the business	

Activity 7

The correct answer is B.

All of the statements except B are correct, which certainly does not apply to private companies which are not allowed by law to market their shares. Many, but not all, public companies apply for a Stock Exchange listing so that a market may be created in their shares. However, even when a public company applies for a Stock Exchange listing, the granting of such a listing does not define when the company comes into existence.

Activity 8

The correct answer is B.

As the name ends in Ltd it must be a private limited company.

Activity 9

The correct answer is D.

The other three options are legal requirements of a public limited company.

 Activity 10

The shares may not be offered to the public.	✓
The shares may not be traded on the stock exchange.	✓
The allocation of shares cannot be changed.	
The company must start with shares worth £100 each.	

 Activity 11

In a general partnership the partners are **jointly** liable for the debts of the company. In contrast when business is carried on through a company **limited** by shares, the **company** is fully liable for any debts contracted rather than the shareholders.

A company is a separate **person** at law and if the shareholders have fully paid the amount due on their **shares** they cannot be called upon to make any further contribution. The rules governing the relationship between the company and its shareholders is set down in the company's **Articles of Association**.

 Activity 12

Where a company is sham, established to help avoid contractual obligations	✓
To identify the true nationality of a company	✓
To establish if a disqualified director is participating in the management of a company	✓

Activity 13

The correct answer is D.
All three statements are correct.

Activity 14

The correct answer is B.
Regardless of the actual date of registration, the only date that matters is the date on the certificate of incorporation (1 May 20X6).

Activity 15

Statement	True/False
It is not possible to register a company limited by shares with the same name as a company already on the register.	True
Once on the register, a company limited by shares cannot change its registered office.	False
The articles of association form the agreement of all initial shareholders to create a company	False
The articles of association of a company limited by shares contain the internal regulations of the company.	True

Activity 16

As partners, the liability of Tina and Kirstie for the firm's debts was **joint.**

In order to register a private company limited by shares the partners will need to submit a number of documents to the Registrar of Companies. These include **a statement of capital** and an application form including **the proposed name of the company** and **details of the registered office.**

If the registrar of Companies is satisfied with the documents, he will issue a **Certificate** of Incorporation which enables the company to commence trading **immediately.**

If the company becomes insolvent, Tina and Kirstie will be liable **for any unpaid portion of the price of their shares**.

Activity 17

The correct answer is B.

A private limited company must file its accounts within nine months.

Activity 18

The correct answer is D.

A limited company needs to file all of these.

Activity 19

	✓
Details of income	✓
Details of expenditure	✓
Details of assets owned by the company	✓
Details of liabilities owed by the company	✓
Details of money spent by the company	✓
Details of money received by the company	✓

Activity 20

The correct answer is B.

The Data Protection Act 1998 is concerned with the misuse of information.

Activity 21

The correct answer is A.

As public limited companies are able to sell their shares to the public, they will often find it easier to raise large amounts of capital for growth, if needed. This may be much harder for partnerships and sole traders. Only public companies can sell shares to the public, companies may be owned by only one shareholder and shareholders enjoy limited liability.

Activity 22

The correct answer is C.

A limited liability company is classed as a separate legal entity from its owners. The owners (shareholders) may be different to the managers (Board of Directors). A shareholder's liability is limited to their investment.

A partnership is different to a limited company in that there is no separate legal entity.

Sole traders have unlimited liability for business debts as they are classed as the same legal entity as the business.

There is no restriction on the number of partners in a partnership agreement

 Activity 23

The statement provided is true.

KAPLAN PUBLISHING

Introduction to Business and Company Law Mock Assessment

Introduction

The following is a Mock Assessment to be attempted in exam conditions.

You should attempt and aim to complete EVERY task.

Each task is independent. You will not need to refer to your answers to previous tasks.

Read every task carefully to make sure you understand what is required.

Where the date is relevant, it is given in the task.

1 Mock Assessment Questions AQ16

Task 1 – The English Legal System – 5 marks

a) Show whether the following statements are true or false.

Statement	True	False
Public law is the law that governs the relationship between individual members of society.		
In civil law the person who sues is called the claimant.		
A court order to carry out a specific performance is an equitable remedy.		

(3 marks)

b) Identify which TWO of the following are examples of delegated legislation

	Delegated legislation?
Statutory instrument	
Act of Parliament	
Case law	
Bye-law	

(2 marks)

KAPLAN PUBLISHING

Task 2 – Contract Formation and Contract Terms – 25 marks

a)   An offer can only be made in writing.

Is this statement true or false?   _____

(1 mark)

b)   Identify which of the following must be present to form a valid contract.

	✓
Warranty	
Consideration	
Invitation to treat	
Agreement	
Intention to create legal relations	
Counter-offer	

(3 marks)

c)   In contract law, are the following statements true or false?

Statement	True	False
An offer cannot be revoked if part payment has been made.		
An offer can never lapse.		
Acceptance must be unconditional.		

(3 marks)

d)   Mendips Stationers Ltd takes a telephone order from a customer for 5 boxes of A4 paper at £5.50 each.

Which of the following statements is correct?

	✓
The customer's order is an invitation to treat and if Mendips Ltd accept the invitation there will be a valid contract.	
The customer's order is an acceptance and if Mendips Ltd agrees there will be an agreement.	
The customer's order is an offer and if Mendips Ltd accept the offer this will form an agreement.	
The customer's order is not valid because it has not been received in writing.	

(3 marks)

e) Shepley Solicitors ask Slip Slop Painters to provide a quotation to paint the reception area of their offices. An estimator costs up the job and gives a quotation of £750.

Shepley Solicitors agree to this price and Slip Slop Painters start the job. Before the job is completed, Slip Slop Painters inform Shepley Solicitors that the quotation was incorrect and they need another £250 to complete the job.

Identify which of the following statements is correct.

	✓
Shepley Solicitors must pay the additional £250 because Slip Slop Painters made a valid mistake.	
Slip Slop Painters cannot force Shepley Solicitors to pay the additional £250 because the agreement was for £750.	
Shepley Solicitors did not send their acceptance in writing so they must pay the full £1,000.	
If Shepley Solicitors do not pay the additional £250, Slip Slop Painters can leave when they have completed work to the value of £750.	

(3 marks)

f) Mr Bones agrees to lend his holiday cottage in Cumbria to a friend for the weekend.

Mr Bones makes sure that the cottage is cleaned and that there is a welcome pack of tea and coffee and some basic foodstuffs in the kitchen.

On the Friday evening, Mr Bones' friend telephones him to say that he cannot now make it due to a family emergency.

Identify which of the following statements is correct.

	✓
Mr Bones can sue his friend for loss of time and expenses incurred because a legal contract was formed.	
This would be considered to be a social and domestic agreement and therefore there was no intention to create a legally binding contract.	
Mr Bones' friend must go to the holiday cottage at the next available opportunity.	

(2 marks)

g) Identify which of the contracts listed below is a valid, void, or voidable contract.

	Valid	Void	Voidable
A contract made between two parties for one to provide transport to smuggle illegal drugs into the UK.			
Goods supplied to a customer on receipt of a purchase order.			
A contract for the sale of property when the seller is of unsound mind.			

(3 marks)

h) Identify whether these statements relate to express terms or implied terms.

Statement	Express term	Implied term
A term which is not specifically stated but still part of the contract because of custom or law.		
A specifically stated term which is described in a contract.		

(2 marks)

i) Identify whether these statements are true or false.

Statement	True	False
Breach of a warranty can entitle the injured party to end the contract.		
Breach of a condition can entitle the injured party to end the contract.		

(2 marks)

j) Rahim had some money stolen from his locker whilst using the swimming pool at his local gym. A notice was displayed on the wall of the changing room which excluded the company from all liability for items lost or stolen whilst on the premises, unless handed to the receptionist for safe keeping.

Which of the following statements is true?

	✓
The liability notice is effective and will exclude the gym from all liability for Rahim's loss.	
Liability notices must be seen before or at the time of entry into the contract. Rahim should have been shown the notice when he registered with the gym. The notice is not effective and Rahim can claim for his loss.	
The contract would have been entered into when Rahim first used the leisure facilities, in this case when he entered the swimming pool. The clause would therefore be incorporated into the contract.	
The notice would be invalid under Unfair Contract Terms Act 1977 and thus unenforceable.	

(3 marks)

Task 3 – Discharging a contract – 10 marks

In each of the following sentences circle the correct option.

a) A breach of contract which occurs on the date the performance is due is **actual/anticipatory** breach.

(1 mark)

b) An express anticipatory breach occurs when one of the parties **declares/does something to show** that the contract will not be completed. (1 mark)

c) Where there is an anticipatory breach of contract, the injured party entitled to sue

after a reasonable time/

from the date the other party indicates their intention not to complete the contract/

from the date the other party fails to perform their part of the contract.

(2 marks)

d) The following statements describe when frustration occurs. Select the correct statement from those provided.

	✓
Frustration occurs where a party fails to perform his contractual obligations due to an event that is beyond the control of either party.	
Frustration occurs where one party breaches his contractual obligations due to interference from the other party.	
Frustration occurs where one party cannot perform his contractual obligations due to his own negligent act.	
Frustration occurs where contractual performance becomes more difficult.	

(3 marks)

e) Which one of the following statements is NOT true?

	✓
Where the defendant maliciously breaches a contract, the court may increase the award of damages to take into account his behaviour.	
Contractual damages are not designed to punish the defendant.	
Generally, a claimant cannot recover damages for losses sustained to a third party.	
The claimant cannot recover more than he actually lost.	

(3 marks)

Task 4 – Employment Law – 20 marks

You may need to refer to this information to answer questions in this section:

Notice periods

Under the Employment Rights Act 1996 (ERA 1996), reasonable notice is determined according to the length of an employee's continuous employment with the same employer as follows:

Length of continuous employment	Statutory minimum notice period
Between 1 month and 2 years	1 week
Between 2 and 12 years	1 week for each year of continuous employment
12 years or more	12 weeks minimum

Redundancy pay

Individuals may be eligible for redundancy pay if certain conditions are met. If these conditions are met, they will receive:

- 1 ½ week's pay for each year of employment after their 41st birthday.
- 1 week's pay for each year of employment after their 22nd birthday.
- ½ week's pay for each year of employment up to their 22nd birthday from the age of 18.

a)   Which ONE of the following tests is NOT used to determine if someone is employed or self-employed?

	✓
Control test	
Services test	
Integration test	
Economic reality test	

(3 marks)

b)   Which of the following could be said to indicate self-employment?

	✓
The employer consistently provides the same amount of supplies each week and expects to pick up roughly the same number of completed products each week.	
The employer does not have to provide work, and the worker can turn down work, but the worker must be available for possible work during specific periods of time.	
The employer provides work when it chooses to and the employee can refuse that work any time, for any reason, although in practice the employer offers work less often to workers who turn down offers of work.	
The parties have no mutual obligations, but the worker will be disciplined for not coming in to work, and the employer has never failed to have work available.	

(3 marks)

c) Show whether the following statements are likely to be true for an employed person or a self-employed person.

Statement	Employed	Self-employed
An individual who is contracted to work 5 days a week from 9am to 5pm with an hour's break for lunch.		
An individual who is contracted to complete work within a specified deadline but who does not have to attend a place of work at a specified time.		

(2 marks)

d) An employee works under a **contract of service / contract for services.**

Circle the correct option from the options provided.

(1 mark)

e) Show whether each of the following statements would indicate employment or self-employment for an individual.

Statement	Employment	Self-employment
The individual is entitled to statutory maternity pay.		
The individual receives gross pay with no deductions.		
The individual receives holiday pay.		

(3 marks)

f) Which TWO of the following are duties of an employee?

	✔
To give honest and faithful service to the employer	
To provide a reference for the employer	
To not misuse confidential information	
To ensure work is delegated	

(2 marks)

g) Huzaifah, who is 28 years old has been working for Clancy Computers for 8 years.

Unfortunately, due to competition in this industry, Huzaifah's job has been made redundant.

His current annual salary is £16,120

How much redundancy pay will Huzaifah get, if all conditions are met?

	✓
£2,015	
£3,100	
£2,480	
£2,170	

(3 marks)

h) Which ONE of the following is the duty of an employer?

	✓
To provide a positive reference to all employees	
To pay at least national minimum wage or national living wage	
To provide transport to and from the place of employment	
To ensure all employees in the accounting department receive AAT training.	

(3 marks)

Task 5 – Employment Law (Dismissal/Redundancy) – 10 marks

a) Identify whether in the following circumstances there is automatically fair reason for dismissal or whether there is potentially fair reason for dismissal.

	Automatically fair reason for dismissal	Potentially fair reason for dismissal
Sam has been making a lot of mistakes in her job. Her employers have provided training courses but her work has not improved.		
Mike has been unhappy about the lack of overtime available due to a downturn in sales. He has encouraged his colleagues to go on strike without informing his trade union representative		
Stacey works as a customs officer at an airport terminal. Her employment was subject to counter-terrorism clearance. The clearance wasn't given before her employment start date, and subsequently the clearance was denied.		
Oz successfully completed the application process. However, it was later discovered that he had falsified his qualifications.		

(4 marks)

b) Identify whether the following statements are true or false in relation to the unfair dismissal process.

Statement	True	False
The employer must serve a grievance notice on the employee.		
The employee must have been continuously employed for two years.		
The claim must go to the tribunal within three months of dismissal.		

(3 marks)

KAPLAN PUBLISHING

c) State whether the following statements are true or false in relation to redundancy.

Statement	True	False
The employer must give an adequate period of consultation before making an employee redundant.		
The employee must have been employed for at least 6 months before redundancy can be offered.		
An employee who is offered a new job with similar terms to the old job within four weeks of the old contract expiring may still take redundancy pay.		

(3 marks)

Task 6 – Company Law – 13 marks

a) Select whether the following statements are true or false in relation to the effects of limited liability and the consequences of incorporation for a company.

Statement	True	False
Limited liability means that all the shareholders are liable for the debts of the company.		
A company is a legal person.		
To become an incorporated company, the business should be registered with HMRC.		

(3 marks)

b) The following statements refer to the veil of corporation. Which statements are true and which are false?

Statement	True	False
It is the name for a type of contract when an individual is a director of more than one company.		
It is when shareholders may be held personally liable for a company's acts.		
It is when limited accounts are prepared for sole traders.		

(3 marks)

c) Show which of the following statements relate to a sole trader, a company, or a general partnership by ticking the boxes provided.

	Sole trader	Company	General partnership
The owner can sue or can be sued for breach of contract.			
The business is a separate legal entity to the owners.			
Each owner is jointly or severally liable for the debts of the business			

(3 marks)

d) The following statements refer to Limited Liability Partnerships. Tick the boxes to mark the correct statements from the list.

Statement	✔
A Limited Liability Partnership is a separate legal entity.	
Each partner is severally responsible for all the other partners' debts.	
A Limited Liability Partnership must register with Companies House.	
A Limited Liability Partnership need not submit a confirmation statement to Companies House.	

(4 marks)

Task 7 – Company Law – 17 marks

a) Match the definition with the document.

Definition	Document

Definition

This document is issued by Companies House and is evidence that the company has been registered.

This is the agreement made by all the initial shareholders when the company was created.

This document is sent to Companies House every year. It is used to check the information that is held on the Companies House register is correct.

Document

Confirmation Statement

Memorandum of Association

Certificate of Incorporation

(3 marks)

b) The following statements concern 'off the shelf' companies. Identify whether the statements are true or false.

Statement	True	False
It is more expensive to set up an 'off the shelf' company than to go through the normal procedure.		
An off-shelf company can only start trading one month after it has been incorporated.		

(2 marks)

c) Before completing the registration process to establish a new business called Gillespie Traders Ltd, the director William Bones enters into a contract for painting the offices.

Who will be liable if the goods were not paid for?

Statement	✔
The members of Gillespie Ltd	
Gillespie Traders Ltd	
William Bones personally	

(3 marks)

d) Identify if the following statements are true or false.

Statement	True	False
You must include your company's name on all company documents, publicity and letters.		
On business letters, order forms and websites, you must show the company's registered number and its registered office address.		

(2 marks)

e) Private limited companies must file their accounts with Companies House. Within which period must this occur?

Tick the correct option from the list provided.

Period of time	✔
Six months after the accounting period	
One year after the accounting period	
Nine months after the accounting period	
Three months after the accounting period	

(3 marks)

f) Private limited companies are required to pay Corporation Tax.

Within which period should a Ltd company pay the Corporation Tax due?

Tick the correct option from the list provided.

Period of time	✓
Every three months	
Nine months and one day after the accounting period	
Nine months after the accounting period	
One year after the accounting period	

(3 marks)

g) Complete the following sentence relating to accounting records by selecting the correct words from those provided in the pick list below:

Accounting records must normally be kept for at least _____ from the end of the financial year they relate to.

Choose from the following options:

1 year
6 years
10 years

(1 mark)

Mock Assessment Answers

1 Mock Assessment Answers

Task 1

a) Show whether the following statements are true or false.

Statement	True	False
Public law is the law that governs the relationship between individual members of society.		✓
In civil law the person who sues is called the claimant.	✓	
A court order to carry out a specific performance is an equitable remedy.	✓	

b) Identify which TWO of the following are examples of delegated legislation

	Delegated legislation?
Statutory instrument	✓
Act of Parliament	
Case law	
Bye-law	✓

Task 2

a)   An offer can only be made in writing. This statement is **FALSE.**

b)   Identify which of the following must be present to form a valid contract.

Warranty	
Consideration	✓
Invitation to treat	
Agreement	✓
Intention to create legal relations	✓
Counter-offer	

c)   In contract law, are the following statements true or false?

Statement	True	False
An offer cannot be revoked if part payment has been made	✓	
An offer can never lapse		✓
Acceptance must be unconditional	✓	

d)   Mendips Stationers Ltd takes a telephone order from a customer for 5 boxes of A4 paper at £5.50 each.

Which of the following statements is correct?

The customer's order is an invitation to treat and if Mendips Ltd accept the invitation there will be a valid contract.	
The customer's order is an acceptance and if Mendips Ltd agrees there will be an agreement.	
The customer's order is an offer and if Mendips Ltd accept the offer this will form an agreement.	✓
The customer's order is not valid because it has not been received in writing	

e)   Shepley Solicitors ask Slip Slop Painters to provide a quotation to paint the reception area of their offices. An estimator costs up the job and gives a quotation of £750.

Shepley Solicitors agree to this price and Slip Slop Painters start the job.   Before the job is completed, Slip Slop Painters inform Shepley Solicitors that the quotation was incorrect and they need another £250 to complete the job.

Shepley Solicitors must pay the additional £250 because Slip Slop Painters made a valid mistake.	
Slip Slop Painters cannot force Shepley Solicitors to pay the additional £250 because the agreement was for £750.	✔
Shepley Solicitors did not send their acceptance in writing so they must pay the full £1,000.	
If Shepley Solicitors do not pay the additional £250, Slip Slop Painters can leave when they have completed work to the value of £750.	

f) Mr Bones agrees to lend his holiday cottage in Cumbria to a friend for the weekend.

Mr Bones makes sure that the cottage is cleaned and that there is a welcome pack of tea and coffee and some basic foodstuffs in the kitchen.

On the Friday evening, Mr Bones' friend telephones him to say that he cannot now make it due to a family emergency.

Mr Bones can sue his friend for loss of time and expenses incurred because a legal contract was formed.	
This would be considered to be a social and domestic agreement and therefore there was no intention to create a legally binding contract.	✔
Mr Bones' friend must go to the holiday cottage at the next available opportunity.	

g)

	Valid	Void	Voidable
A contract made between two parties for one to provide transport to smuggle illegal drugs into the UK.		✔	
Goods supplied to a customer on receipt of a purchase order.	✔		
A contract for the sale of property when the seller is of unsound mind.			✔

h)

Statement	Express term	Implied term
A term which is not specifically stated but still part of the contract because of custom or law.		✓
A specifically stated term which is described in a contract.	✓	

i) Identify whether these statements are true or false.

Statement	True	False
Breach of a warranty can entitle the injured party to end the contract.		✓
Breach of a condition can entitle the injured party to end the contract.	✓	

j) Rahim had some money stolen from his locker whilst using the swimming pool at his local gym. A notice was displayed on the wall of the changing room which excluded the company from all liability for items lost or stolen whilst on the premises, unless handed to the receptionist for safe keeping.

The liability notice is effective and will exclude the gym from all liability for Rahim's loss.	
Liability notices must be seen before or at the time of entry into the contract. Rahim should have been shown the notice when he registered with the gym. The notice is not effective and Rahim can claim for his loss.	✓
The contract would have been entered into when Rahim first used the leisure facilities, in this case when he entered the swimming pool. The clause would therefore be incorporated into the contract.	
The notice would be invalid under Unfair Contract Terms Act 1977 and thus unenforceable.	

Task 3

a) A breach of contract which occurs on the date the performance is due is **actual** breach.

b) An express anticipatory breach occurs when one of the parties **declares** that the contract will not be completed.

c) Where there is an anticipatory breach of contract, the injured party entitled to sue **from the date the other party indicates their intention not to complete the contract.**

d) The following statements describe when frustration occurs. Select the correct statement from those provided.

Frustration occurs where a party fails to perform his contractual obligations due to an event that is beyond the control of either party.	✔
Frustration occurs where one party breaches his contractual obligations due to interference from the other party.	
Frustration occurs where one party cannot perform his contractual obligations due to his own negligent act.	
Frustration occurs where contractual performance becomes more difficult.	

e) Which one of the following statements is NOT true?

Where the defendant maliciously breaches a contract, the court may increase the award of damages to take into account his behaviour.	✔
Contractual damages are not designed to punish the defendant.	
Generally, a claimant cannot recover damages for losses sustained to a third party.	
The claimant cannot recover more than he actually lost.	

Task 4

a) Which ONE of the following tests is NOT used to determine if someone is employed or self-employed?

Control test	
Services test	✓
Integration test	
Economic reality test	

b) Which of the following could be said to indicate self-employment?

The employer consistently provides the same amount of supplies each week and expects to pick up roughly the same number of completed products each week.	
The employer does not have to provide work, and the worker can turn down work, but the worker must be available for possible work during specific periods of time.	
The employer provides work when it chooses to and the employee can refuse that work any time, for any reason, although in practice the employer offers work less often to workers who turn down offers of work.	✓
The parties have no mutual obligations, but the worker will be disciplined for not coming in to work, and the employer has never failed to have work available.	

c)

Statement	Employed	Self-employed
An individual who is contracted to work 5 days a week from 9am to 5pm with an hour's break for lunch.	✓	
An individual who is contracted to complete work within a specified deadline but who does not have to attend a place of work at a specified time.		✓

d) An employee works under a **contract of service.**

e)

Statement	Employment	Self-employment
The individual is entitled to statutory maternity pay.	✓	
The individual receives gross pay with no deductions.		✓
The individual receives holiday pay.	✓	

f) Which TWO of the following are duties of an employee?

To give honest and faithful service to the employer	✓
To provide a reference for the employer	
To not misuse confidential information	✓
To ensure work is delegated	

g) Huzaifah, who is 28 years old, has been working for Clancy Computers for 8 years.

Unfortunately, due to competition in this industry, Huzaifah's job has been made redundant.

His current annual salary is £16,120

How much redundancy pay will Huzaifah get, if all conditions are met?

£2,015	
£3,100	
£2,480	
£2,170	✓

h) Which ONE of the following is the duty of an employer?

To provide a positive reference to all employees	
To pay at least national minimum wage or national living wage	✓
To provide transport to and from the place of employment	
To ensure all employees in the accounting department receive AAT training.	

Task 5

a)

	Automatically fair reason for dismissal	Potentially fair reason for dismissal
Sam has been making a lot of mistakes in her job. Her employers have provided training courses but her work has not improved.		✓
Mike has been unhappy about the lack of overtime available due to a downturn in sales. He has encouraged his colleagues to go on strike without informing his trade union representative	✓	
Stacey works as a customs officer at an airport terminal. Her employment was subject to counter-terrorism clearance. The clearance wasn't given before her employment start date, and subsequently the clearance was denied.	✓	
Oz successfully completed the application process. However, it was later discovered that he had falsified his qualifications.		✓

b)   Identify whether the following statements are true or false in relation to the unfair dismissal process.

Statement	True	False
The employer must serve a grievance notice on the employee.		✓
The employee must have been continuously employed for two years.	✓	
The claim must go to the tribunal within three months of dismissal.	✓	

c) State whether the following statements are true or false in relation to redundancy.

Statement	True	False
The employer must give an adequate period of consultation before making an employee redundant.	✓	
The employee must have been employed for at least 6 months before redundancy can be offered.		✓
An employee who is offered a new job with similar terms to the old job within four weeks of the old contract expiring may still take redundancy pay.		✓

Task 6

a)

Statement	True	False
Limited liability means that all the shareholders are liable for the debts of the company.		✓
A company is a legal person.	✓	
To become an incorporated company, the business should be registered with HMRC.		✓

b) The following statements refer to the veil of corporation. Which statements are true and which are false?

Statement	True	False
It is the name for a type of contract when an individual is a director of more than one company.		✓
It is when shareholders may be held personally liable for a company's acts.	✓	
It is when limited accounts are prepared for sole traders.		✓

KAPLAN PUBLISHING

c) Show which of the following statements relate to a sole trader, a company, or a general partnership by ticking the boxes provided.

	Sole trader	Company	General partnership
The owner can sue or can be sued for breach of contract.	✓		
The business is a separate legal entity to the owners.		✓	
Each owner is jointly or severally liable for the debts of the business			✓

d) The following statements refer to Limited Liability Partnerships. Tick the boxes to mark the correct statements from the list.

A Limited Liability Partnership is a separate legal entity.	✓
Each partner is severally responsible for all the other partners' debts.	
A Limited Liability Partnership must register with Companies House.	✓
A Limited Liability Partnership need not submit a confirmation statement to Companies House.	

Task 7

a) Match the definition with the document.

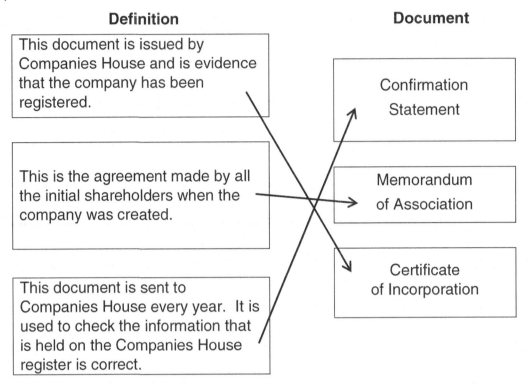

Definition

This document is issued by Companies House and is evidence that the company has been registered.

This is the agreement made by all the initial shareholders when the company was created.

This document is sent to Companies House every year. It is used to check the information that is held on the Companies House register is correct.

Document

Confirmation Statement

Memorandum of Association

Certificate of Incorporation

b) The following statements concern 'off the shelf' companies. Identify whether the statements are true or false.

Statement	True	False
It is more expensive to set up an 'off the shelf' company than to go through the normal procedure.		✔
An off-shelf company can only start trading one month after it has been incorporated.		✔

c) Before completing the registration process to establish a new business called Gillespie Traders Ltd, the director William Bones enters into a contract for painting the offices.

Who will be liable if the goods were not paid for?

The members of Gillespie Ltd	
Gillespie Traders Ltd	
William Bones personally	✔

d) Identify if the following statements are true or false.

Statement	True	False
You must include your company's name on all company documents, publicity and letters.	✓	
On business letters, order forms and websites, you must show the company's registered number and its registered office address.	✓	

e) Private limited companies must file their accounts with Companies House. Within which period must this occur?

Six months after the accounting period	
One year after the accounting period	
Nine months after the accounting period	✓
Three months after the accounting period	

f) Private limited companies are required to pay Corporation Tax.

Within which period should a Ltd company pay the Corporation Tax due?

Every three months	
Nine months and one day after the accounting period	✓
Nine months after the accounting period	
One year after the accounting period	

g) Accounting records must normally be kept for at least **6 years** from the end of the financial year they relate to.

INDEX

KAPLAN PUBLISHING

KAPLAN PUBLISHING

KAPLAN PUBLISHING